HELL
WEEK

HELL WEEK

SEVEN DAYS TO BE
YOUR BEST SELF

ERIK BERTRAND LARSSEN

GALLERY BOOKS

New York   London   Sydney   Toronto   New Delhi

This publication contains the opinions and ideas of its author. It is intended to provide helpful and informative material on the subjects addressed in the publication. It is sold with the understanding that the author and publisher are not engaged in rendering medical, health, or any other kind of personal professional services in the book. The reader should consult his or her medical, health, or other competent professional before adopting any of the suggestions in this book or drawing inferences from it.

The author and publisher specifically disclaim all responsibility for any liability, loss, or risk, personal or otherwise, which is incurred as a consequence, directly or indirectly, of the use and application of any of the contents of this book.

Gallery Books
An Imprint of Simon & Schuster, Inc.
1230 Avenue of the Americas
New York, NY 10020

Copyright © 2013 by J.M. Stenersens Forlag AS
English language translation copyright © 2016 by Erik Bertrand Larssen
Written in collaboration with Torbjørn Lysebo Ekelund
Originally published in Norway in 2013 as *Helvetesuka*

First Gallery Books hardcover edition June 2016

GALLERY BOOKS and colophon are registered trademarks
of Simon & Schuster, Inc.

For information about special discounts for bulk purchases,
please contact Simon & Schuster Special Sales at 1-866-506-1949
or business@simonandschuster.com.

The Simon & Schuster Speakers Bureau can bring authors
to your live event. For more information or to book an event,
contact the Simon & Schuster Speakers Bureau at 1-866-248-3049
or visit our website at www.simonspeakers.com.

Interior design by Renato Stanisic

Manufactured in the United States of America

10 9 8 7 6 5 4 3 2 1

Library of Congress Cataloging-in-Publication Data is available.

ISBN 978-1-4767-8336-9
ISBN 978-1-4767-8339-0 (ebook)

For my beautiful wife, Louise—
You have the most generous heart and the most caring soul.
Thank you for inspiring me every day. I love you.

CONTENTS

INTRODUCTION

IF YOU ARE GOING THROUGH HELL, KEEP GOING. —WINSTON S. CHURCHILL

My career as a mental trainer officially started a decade ago, but the seed was planted much earlier, when I was a nineteen-year-old student in the Norwegian Officer Candidate School for the Cavalry. The fact that I'd been admitted to the school at all was somewhat of a miracle, since growing up I wasn't exactly what you'd call army material. Just the opposite: I was the scrawny kid who got pushed around a lot on the playground and had trouble connecting with his peers.

Fortunately, I had a family who loved and supported me, which meant that I still developed a sense of self-esteem even though I was scrawny. Eventually I also developed physically, but what impressed Norway's military recruiters was my internal qualities—my attitude. I was even being considered for the Recon unit, the most sought after at the school (and a precursor to my becoming a paratrooper two years later with the Norwegian special forces, trained to operate deep behind enemy lines, much like the United States Special Forces Airborne units).

So there I was, seated in a classroom for my first lecture on wilderness survival. This is an essential skill for any military personnel, but especially for Recons, given the risky nature of their missions. They often find themselves in situations where they're forced to fend for themselves—say, if an operation goes awry or if they escape enemy capture and need to find their way back to the unit without the benefit of navigation aids.

I looked around at the other students in the class, all of whom seemed even stronger and more confident than I had become as a young man, and I wondered if I'd bitten off more than I could chew.

That's when the officer at the head of the class took a piece of chalk and drew a vertical line on an empty blackboard. He then plotted the numbers zero through ten along the line in ascending order, zero at the bottom and ten on top.

He pointed to the number four and said, "This is how much you think you can take." Then he pointed to the number two and said, "Your mother probably thinks you can take only this much." He moved his index finger gradually up to seven. "The officers in this room know you can take a lot more." He looked at us sternly.

"But here's the reality. You can take even more than they think." His index finger stopped at ten. "Most importantly, you can take a lot more than *you* think."

You can take a lot more than you think.

Those words stuck with me that day, as my fellow soldiers and I moved from the classroom to the mess hall to the barracks. Lying in bed that night, I pondered the simplicity of the officer's statement, but also its enormity. It seemed to contain one of the great secrets of life.

The next morning, I was up before dawn with the rest of my unit, eager to swiftly move up the vertical axis. I pushed myself to the furthest edge of my limits during that survival training. Never before had I walked such long distances without food in my stomach, or swam so much in freezing cold waters. Never before had I navigated solely by the position of the stars or built a fire using only sticks and the hemp from a section of rope.

With each new accomplishment, more of my best was revealed. I realized that just as the officer had predicted, I could take on much more than I ever thought possible. That revelation, which started with the officer's words and played out over the course of my survival training, changed my life forever—and it would ultimately lead to my career as a mental trainer.

First, though, I had to fulfill my military duty, serving as a leader in the long-range reconnaissance and paratrooper units. That is, until my career and nearly my life were cut short by an automobile accident (but we'll get to that later). I came back, though, and my military experience took me to Afghanistan, Kosovo, Bosnia, Macedonia, and many other missions for the military in between. I trained and fought alongside the British Special Air Service. These formative years opened my eyes to the values—hard work, decisiveness, character—that I hold dear, both as an individual and as a mental trainer.

After retiring from the military, I needed a different kind of challenge, so I decided to enter the world of business—which of course has its own kind of battlefields and war zones. Armed with a master's degree from the Norwegian School of

Economics and Business Administration, I worked in finance and for a company that specialized in recruitment and management development.

It was during that stage of my career that I witnessed first-hand the career frustrations that so many people experience on a daily basis. More often than not, it was obvious that they were holding *themselves* back, not anyone else. What's more, they seemed to understand this. There was the corporate manager who knew that he needed to be more structured with his job. He knew he had to plan more efficiently for meetings with his staff, to articulate ideas more clearly to clients, and to impress his own superiors with a more convincing semblance of order or control. With all those shortcomings, it's a wonder he managed to hold on to his job—though corporations often tolerate mediocrity, at least until it catches up with them and the whole operation comes crashing down.

I met many people in similar situations during those early years in the business world. I've always hung around athletes, and I started to become aware of the same thing there, even at the highest levels, where you'd expect more discipline and commitment. Instead of sticking to a healthy diet, these guys would cheat with pizza or burgers and fries. Instead of getting that much-needed nap in the afternoon, they'd spend the time surfing the Internet. Just like the middling corporate manager, the underachieving athletes I mixed with recognized the error of their ways. They just couldn't break away from the bad habits. Even when they had the know-how and the resources to do better, they chose the path of least resistance.

Then there were the exceptions, the winners and the over-achievers and the leaders of their fields. Perhaps owing to the fact that I was a pretty late bloomer in life, I've always been curious about these people. How do they differ from the rest of us? Where do they find the resolve to plan for every meeting or competition and resist every temptation? Why do they win, exactly?

I began to work on these questions more systematically. I found that the distinctions between the winners and the rest of us are *surprisingly small*. Those who perform at the highest level have one thing in common: they pay attention to detail. They develop exceptional habits, where others settle for the norm. They are better at making more of the small, positive decisions in their everyday life. The sum of all of these choices may not make a difference on a daily basis, but over time—weeks, months, years—the effect is enormous. Since this practice has nothing to do with being born with the right skills, everybody has this opportunity dormant within them. It isn't a question of talent. It's a question of choice.

With that revelation, I knew that I had found my calling. This is what mental training is all about: adjusting your habits today in order to achieve great changes in your future performance over time, and being prepared for situations where you need to perform at the highest level. I have enormous faith in our ability to lead ever better and even perfect lives. At the very least, we're able to constantly strive for that level of perfection, or self-actualization, as it's sometimes called.

As I made the move into mental training, this became my mission: to help others get really good at living their lives. Of course this looks different depending on the individual. For some, the goal is to perform at the highest possible level in a variety of arenas, including the work and family spheres. For others, including top athletes, it means achieving excellence at just one thing. Either way, the process for getting there is the same. It's all about making the key changes.

But how? That was the next question I considered. How do I convince people of their capacity to change? How do I get them to discover their best selves? That's when I came back to Hell Week. Anytime I get together with ex-military people, whether guys I served with or total strangers, at some point the conversation turns to Hell Week. Everyone who goes through the experience carries it with them for the rest of their lives. They talk about specific instances from the week with exacting detail. Often it has to do with the breaking point that they went right up to, but somehow managed to resist. Decades later, the resilience they discovered during that moment of extreme adversity is still core to their being. In short, the lessons of Hell Week last a lifetime.

That's certainly true for me. As I thought more deeply about the structure of Hell Week, I realized it could be easily applied to civilian life. Of course, you see versions of it in the real world—think of college fraternities with their week of hazing for incoming pledges. From what I hear, that Hell Week can be a little sadistic, even by military standards, and it's probably not the most positive influence.

The civilian Hell Week that I began to envision would have at its core the principle I learned all those years ago: *You can take a lot more than you think.* The challenge is stepping outside your normal routine in a way that allows you to unlock your deep reserves of untapped potential. This is what my Hell Week is all about.

I often cite the number 4,160. That's the total number of

weeks you'll live if you reach the age of eighty. Most of them zip by in a blur. There are the demands of everyday life—from preparing meals to paying bills to social, familial, and parental responsibilities. In our professional lives, weeks are jammed with emails, phone calls, and meeting after meeting. Sure, there are the vacations to break up the routine, but they're all about escaping real life, rather than examining it up close.

Hell Week is an opportunity to apply the principles of mental training in a fixed time frame. For seven days, starting at five o'clock Monday morning and ending at ten o'clock Sunday night, you will live your life to the highest possible caliber. You will push yourself in ways you never thought possible. You will replace your old self with a new and improved version.

Can people really change their lives in a single week? I often meet with skeptics, who point to studies suggesting it can take several months for new habits to form. I don't dispute that, and in fact, I make the point clearly to clients that Hell Week is the beginning of a process, not the end. But I do strongly believe that if you apply yourself seriously to the project, your life will be changed for the better.

Hell Week is not about torturing yourself to achieve a goal. It's being fully present, whether you're leading a meeting at the office or studying hard for an exam. It's finding balance between the various spheres in which you operate. It's giving to others and being a good person. It's about coping with life, understanding life, and living life to the maximum potential.

THE SEVEN DAYS OF HELL WEEK

This book will walk you step by step through the regimen my clients follow so that you can achieve not only what you already know you should be doing, but more than you ever dreamed of. Each day has a different theme and area of focus, which I will dive into more deeply later in the book. But to give you an idea of the challenges you'll face as you proceed from Monday morning to Sunday night, what follows is a brief overview of the week. I should stress that Hell Week should be done during a routine week in your life. You should go to work as normal and tend to all the demands of your home and family life. The only difference is you will be executing those tasks to the highest level, while taking on the added challenges of Hell Week. It will not be easy. But I promise you it will be exciting and rewarding.

MONDAY: HABITS

This day will be devoted to figuring out which habits are helping you and which are holding you back. There's an old saying, "Habits are cobwebs at first, cables at last." You'll start creating good habits today that will be with you years from now. Remember: you determine your habits, they don't determine you.

TUESDAY: MOOD AND FOCUS

How many moods do you have in a given day? Are you bringing the right moods to the right situations? Tuesday of Hell Week answers these questions by being hyperfocused on your state of mind. You'll learn how to take charge of your moods and bring the right energy to the day's various events and interactions.

WEDNESDAY: TIME MANAGEMENT

The modern world seems to conspire against time management at every turn. On Wednesday, you'll learn how to fight back with thorough planning and preparation. Creating clear goals, maintaining to-do lists, and dividing your life into days, weeks, months, and years are among the tasks you'll tackle.

THURSDAY: THE COMFORT ZONE

If it was supposed to be easy, it wouldn't be called Hell Week. That fact will be apparent on Thursday, the week's toughest day, which gets you outside your comfort zone to discover new limits. For starters, you will not sleep for a full forty-one hours. You will impose a complete social media blackout. You will confront at least one of your deepest fears. It's going to be hell, but I promise you won't regret it.

FRIDAY: REST AND RESTITUTION

A day devoted to the pursuit of real restorative rest will follow Hell Week's hardest day. Rest is not a luxury. It is an essential human need that enables us to function at our highest level. You are probably not doing enough in your regular life to recharge the mind and body. Today you will focus on ways to change that.

SATURDAY: INNER DIALOGUE

Thoughts determine character. By changing your thought patterns, you can effectively change your life. As Hell Week winds down, on Saturday you will channel your thoughts toward the positive. We all have the potential to be our own worst enemy or best ally. On this day, you will learn how to win over your inner dialogue.

SUNDAY: REFLECTION

The final day of Hell Week is an opportunity to look back on everything that you accomplished. You'll need time to sort through the experiences and put your life into perspective, through targeted self-reflection and interactions with key people. You have made a major investment in yourself. On Sunday, make sure it pays off.

Nothing to it, right? Seriously, Hell Week is a major challenge. But having guided hundreds of clients through the program, I can tell you that if you make the commitment and go through the process, you'll come to see that becoming your best possible self isn't as hard as you feared. Small actions have major effects: You will eat healthily, exercise every day, and rest effectively. You will listen to the people around you, work with concentration, get up early, and go to bed early. You will be thorough in everything you undertake, cut out inessentials, and prioritize appropriately. You will be a good fellow human being. You will give. You will be positive and happy. You will be energetic, assertive, proactive, and dynamic. You will be the best version of yourself for one whole week. It's one week that will change your life forever.

Remember: you can take a lot more than you think. Now let's get started.

HOW TO USE
THIS BOOK

The process outlined in this book mirrors the one
I use for my clients. As you move from the planning
phase to the day-by-day guidelines of Hell Week to the
post–Hell Week instruction, you'll be experiencing the
same process I've prescribed to hundreds of business
leaders, top athletes, and other high achievers.

The book is divided into three basic parts:

Part One, "Planning and Preparation," deals with the
planning and prep work, and includes things like gathering
feedback from important people in your life and taking a
hard look at your exercise and eating habits. This process
generally takes two to three weeks.

Part Two, "Here Comes Hell Week," deals with Hell
Week itself, with each day being devoted to a key tenet of
what I sometimes call "The Bertrand Method." You'll work
on mood control one day, time management the next, and
so on.

Part Three, "Life After Hell Week," teaches you how to
apply the lessons of Hell Week to the rest of your life.

When I work directly with clients, no two processes
are the same. Some people take easily to the program and
even end up committing to multiple Hell Weeks throughout
the year. Others go through a period of resistance before
coming around. A handful of clients even decide that Hell
Week isn't right for them. Obviously, I hope you'll go all out

from start to finish, which is how to get the most out of the experience. But my point is that there's no one right way to approach Hell Week. Likewise, there's no one right way to read this book.

You might read it cover to cover before embarking on your Hell Week journey. I love that enthusiasm, and I've kept the book short enough so that a free Sunday or cross-country flight should be enough time to plow through it.

Another option is to take the sections of the book as they occur during your actual Hell Week journey. In other words, read Part One while you're preparing, Part Two while you're in Hell Week, and Part Three in the weeks and months that follow. I like this approach, too, since it encourages you to return time and again to sections of the book that are most relevant to your journey.

That's another important point that I want to emphasize further: everyone's Hell Week is going to look different. For the top athlete, they'll need to focus less on exercise and diet and more, perhaps, on time management or embracing adversity. For the high-powered CEO, the opposite might be true.

I've written this book for everyone, and I've tried to organize the material so that you can find your own best way through it. Whether you move from beginning to end or jump around is entirely up to you. All I ask is that whichever path you choose, you commit to it 100 percent. When it comes to Hell Week, "all out" is the only way to go.

Personal Stories from Hell Week

I have drawn on my experience with my clients to create three typical clients to better illustrate my program, and written journal entries for them in the text that follows. Even if your life situation is very different from that described, I think these stories will help give you a better sense of what Hell Week entails. Here's a little more about each of them:

Dave is a media professional in his early 40s. He and his wife have two young children whom they adore, a lovely home, and many friends. Not a bad life, on the whole. The big issue has to do with work. After Dave moved steadily up the ladder in the publishing industry through the early part of his career, progress has come to a halt in recent years, so he's looking to hit the reset button. In addition to getting out of his professional rut, Dave is eager to get back into shape physically. A lifelong competitive athlete, he has started to feel the effects of middle age—the extra ten pounds or creeping bad eating habits. He knows he'll never run like a twenty-five-year-old, but he would like to return to peak physical fitness, through improved diet and a more committed exercise regimen.

Jillian is a thirtysomething professional who works in the real-estate division of a big bank. On paper, she has it all: a top-tier education, a great family, and a busy social life. And that's how it's always been. Success has come easy. Unfortunately, the older she gets, the harder it is to maintain the high standard. The pressure to say yes to everything and do it perfectly is starting to weigh on her. She wants to find a definition of happiness that's not so entirely dependent on achievement.

She also wants to be better at prioritizing what's important in life.

Adam works in IT, running operations for a big manufacturing company. He's accomplished a lot in his professional life, but it's come at a serious cost to his health. When he first walked through my door, he was probably close to fifty pounds overweight. He's a devoted father, but he's been less and less able to do stuff with his kids because of the extra weight. None of the diets or new exercise regimens he's tried have stuck. He needed something to kick-start his life and thought Hell Week might be the answer.

PART ONE

PLANNING AND PREPARATION

BY FAILING TO PREPARE, YOU ARE PREPARING TO FAIL. —BENJAMIN FRANKLIN

Whom did you worship when you were young? For a lot of people, the answer to that question will be a professional athlete, a famous musician, a favorite writer, or a movie star. When I was young, my biggest heroes were polar explorers—a little unusual, I admit, though remember I grew up in the snowy wilds of Norway, where names like Fridtjof Nansen and Ralph Høibakk (two of our more accomplished adventurers) were as common as your Derek Jeter and LeBron James.

One of my favorite early explorers was the famous Roald Amundsen, who won the race to the South Pole on December 14, 1911, beating out Robert Falcon Scott by thirty-four days. A great deal has been written about that extraordinary contest and the controversy surrounding it. I have enormous respect for both men, but I do believe Amundsen reached the destination first—and I think he did so because of his superior preparation.

Polar expeditions are extremely complex, with a huge number of deciding factors. Some of them can be managed, or at least anticipated, while other factors are completely beyond human control. Amundsen focused on those he could control. For example, he assembled his team with men who had deep knowledge of the polar region and, at the same time, were highly competent craftsmen and skiers. He used dogs instead of Scott's doomed horses. Food rations were precisely calculated, and included calorie-rich cocoa rather than Scott's very British calorie-light tea.

I could go on and on, but you get the point. As the Boy Scouts motto puts it, "Be prepared." I learned that lesson early on through my childhood obsession with polar exploration. In the military, it was hammered home with such maxims as "The person who is prepared survives" and "Attention to detail brings security." Preparation was literally the difference between life or death.

The stakes aren't quite so extreme in the contemporary world, but preparation is still absolutely vital to success. The athletes who perform best in live competition are without exception the ones who know how to get themselves ready in the months, weeks, and minutes leading up to the event. The same goes for business executives, actors, or anyone whose job requires some element of performance (and when you think about it, are there any that don't?). Winners do whatever they need to do in order to increase their likelihood of success.

To win at Hell Week and use the lessons from it to make meaningful improvements to your life, you need to prepare. That's what this section of the book is all about. Together, we're going to make sure that nothing is left to chance. I see people make this mistake all the time. They view preparations as boring or pointless or difficult, and instead they cross their fingers and hope for the best. During Hell Week, you will not rely on hope. You will enter into it knowing that you are going to be successful. That's because you are going to be prepared.

THE SEVEN-STEP PLAN

As I noted in my introduction, you should start getting ready for Hell Week two or three weeks beforehand. This is a crucial period, because it's during this time that you'll build up the momentum and motivation needed for a successful outcome. You won't achieve real and lasting transformation if you don't know exactly which aspects of your life you're looking to change. Remember, it's the small decisions that, when added up, have the greatest impact.

I've devised a seven-step process that will help you define your goals for Hell Week and come up with a plan for achieving them. Think of it this way: Hell Week comprises the actual performance situation, akin to the ten-kilometer race in swimming. We all know that when the starting gun sounds, the swimmers have already undertaken most of the work. They've trained systematically, grinding away at the details, preparing themselves mentally for what lies ahead, visualizing every aspect of the race, picturing various scenarios in their mind, and deciding how they'll respond to the different challenges they'll face along the way. Of course, one of those swimmers will have done all these things more diligently than the rest, and it's his hand that will touch the wall first.

The following seven-step plan will help you bring that same level of preparedness to Hell Week. Some of the steps are action oriented, while others are more contemplative, requiring you to reflect on your life—its past, present, and future. If you don't already keep a journal, I strongly urge you to start one for this process. Throughout the book, you'll see journal entries from my past clients. Like them, you're going to discover a lot about yourself in the weeks to come. You'll want to keep a record of the exploration.

STEP ONE: EMBRACE ADVERSITY

If I had to choose one word that embodies Hell Week and the method behind it, that word would be *adversity*. For soldiers undergoing the military version of the seven-day challenge, it's all about the will to continue. That's why I love that quote from Churchill in the introduction: "If you are going through hell, keep going."

As you get ready for Hell Week, the notion of adversity always should be foremost in your mind. My clients are sometimes confused by this mandate when I first start working with them, since my method is so much about focusing on success. They're confusing failure with adversity. Failure is a negative. Adversity is a positive. Indeed, it's one of the best forms of motivation, provided you're prepared for it.

I once served with a fellow paratrooper whom we called Ice Cube because he loved the cold. Norwegians are, of course, accustomed to frigid conditions, but this guy really seemed to thrive in them. I asked him about this one day and his response was simple. "I'm good at being cold," he said. For whatever reason, Ice Cube was able to withstand cold temperatures much better than other people. It's not that it was easy for him. I watched his teeth chatter and his lips turn blue along with everybody else. But he was able to persevere and see through to the other side of the pain. And this became an incredible motivator for him. Every time he overcame the cold, it provided a sense of achievement and recognition.

During Hell Week, I want you to get good at being cold. I fully believe that it's possible to teach yourself to not just handle adversity, but to truly enjoy it. And through that process, you will build strength and character. It's a great opportunity that so many people miss because they've been conditioned to avoid adversity. Remember, adversity doesn't equal failure. It equals opportunity. Adversity is part of the journey toward a worthwhile goal.

I learned this lesson the hard way one morning in February 1996. I was still in the military, returning to the base from a twenty-four-hour R and R at my family home. The mountain roads were icy, so I was taking it slowly. Around a sharp bend, a bus filled with tourists heading for a skiing holiday slammed into my tiny Renault. Just before impact, I assumed the position we use in parachuting, pulling my legs halfway under my body, hunching my back and neck, and pushing my underarms together and my fists over my head.

A shrill, metallic sound followed, then the violent force of impact—twice, in fact, as the bus spun around and broadsided me a second time. Then all was silent. I sat still for a few seconds and examined my body, patting my legs, my thighs, my stomach, and my chest. I felt intact. I crawled out of the shattered windshield and shifted into military mode, doing my part to secure the scene and tend to injured tourists. Eventually the emergency services arrived.

A policeman approached me and said they were looking for the passengers of my Renault, and pointed to my crumpled wreck of a car. For the first time, I let myself slip down onto the ground. "I think you should come along to the ambulance," the police officer said. The adrenaline seeped out of my body, and all at once I felt the pain in my knee, chest, neck, and head.

Fortunately, miraculously, none of my injuries were serious—a couple of bruised ribs, a mild concussion, and a gash on my knee. I was discharged from the hospital, feeling very lucky, except for the crushing pain in my head and neck.

That's when the real struggle began. The first year after the accident was the toughest of my life. The pain didn't go away. It stayed with me all day, every day. Though I was able to complete my certification as a paratrooper, the pain eventually forced me to leave the military.

I made the decision to study economics at the Norwegian School of Economics and Business Administration, hoping the rigors of academia might distract me from the pain. One day into lectures and the pain had won. I couldn't concentrate. Sleep was fitful at best. I lost my girlfriend. I began to despair and feel sorry for myself. I met with all kinds of specialists, from chiropractors to physiotherapists. My depression only grew deeper. I traveled to Sweden, the United States, and Australia to meet with more specialists. Nothing helped. I started to lose faith and think even darker thoughts.

One day my father called to see how I was doing. I told him the truth, putting it all on the table. "It must be challenging," he said. We talked about this and that, and then he said something unexpected. "Erik, you're in one of these situations where, as they say, the wheat is separated from the chaff. This is where you get to prove what you're made of."

That same day I had a conversation with a minister whom our family had known for years. He, too, asked how I was doing, and again I told the truth. For the second time that day I got a surprising response. "Isn't it fascinating," he said.

"Fascinating?" I answered.

"Yes," he said. "The range of emotion we have inside. It's fascinating. A human being can feel everything from extreme happiness, love, joy, achievement, and safety to the deepest sadness, fear, and misfortune."

In the days that followed I reflected on these two conversations. Slowly, I began to see my situation in a different light. The state of adversity I was in was a kind of challenge. My father's words made me realize that. They got my competitive juices flowing. Would I overcome it or be swallowed whole?

The minister's words, meanwhile, made me think about the inevitable ups and downs of life. I realized that I was on an incredible high before my accident—thriving in the military, being in love with my girlfriend, and forging lots of friendships. Now I was experiencing the opposite. I was in the downturn, and I actually felt lucky to be there. Life becomes stronger and richer when you can feel the ups and downs, and the bad feelings with the good.

With this new perspective, I began to rally. I countered the adversity with small changes, both physical and mental. I began to build up my strength and my powers of concentration, allowing myself longer breaks and rest periods in the beginning. I was in hell. I just needed to keep going.

I began to like adversity. I wanted to win. It took me eleven years to get through business school. The journey was longer and harder than I thought possible. But when I phoned the exams office to learn my final grade on my master's thesis, and the woman on the other end of the line said "A," I burst into tears of happiness.

Today, the experience of my accident and recovery is central to who I am. I wouldn't have gotten where I am without it. I actually feel lucky to have been through the ordeal, because it allowed me to recognize life's ups and downs. I know that whenever darkness descends, I can fight my way back into the light.

That's one of my adversity stories. What are some of yours? That's the question for you to answer during this stage of your Hell Week preparation. Obviously, you're not going to go out and seek to create adversity in your life (especially a horrible car wreck). But I do want you to redefine the meaning and role of adversity in your life.

Remember that anyone can perform well when things are going their way. The difference between the best and the rest is their ability to mobilize in the face of hardship. A businessperson might find motivation by performing well in a tough market. For the athlete, it might be playing through an injury.

On the journey toward your goal, whatever it might be, you always have to expect a downturn. It's essential to have this in mind, because emotions to a large extent are steered by expectations. If you expect your journey to be nothing but fun and games, your emotions will play out differently than if you expect some degree of hardship. And the journey toward your goal will be filled with meaning.

Do this right, and you'll come to welcome the hard times. You'll want life not to be easy all the time, because you'll know that something beautiful is waiting for you at the other end. It could be just a short period of physical training, knowing the rush of endorphins you'll have afterward. It could be putting in that incredibly hard week at work, knowing the intense feeling of reward it will bring on Friday. Through a full-scale embrace of adversity, you will come to appreciate the fullness of life.

THE ACTION PLAN

Take stock. I always ask my clients to list the ups and downs in their lives. The highs include their proudest accomplishments and happiest moments. The lows might include the loss of a job or the end of a relationship. The point of this exercise is to simply make you recognize the peaks and valleys that are part of life. By accepting that fact, you'll be less likely to fall into a state of despair and self-pity when bad things happen. Instead, you'll see them as a simple matter of course and take the steps necessary to move past them.

Look for the lesson. Adversity is an opportunity to grow stronger and learn something new about who you are as a person, but you first need to be able to see the challenges in life as teachable moments. To do so, it helps to recognize the fact that negative states are temporary (as are positive ones). "This, too, shall pass" is the old adage. In that mind-set, you'll have an easier time analyzing the adversity, understanding how you ended up in the situation, and figuring out what you need to do to get out of it.

Share your pain. Thinking back on my own adversity story, the period following my accident when I was locked in my own head was the darkest. As soon as I confided in my father and minister, the darkness began to lift. Make a list of people you know you can turn to when the going gets tough. Knowing that you have a network and a support system in place will help you prepare for adversity. That's especially true if your network is filled with positive people. Remember that it's a two-way street. You need to be there when someone from your support system is dealing with adversity. As you get better at this, you'll learn to recognize when they're in that state, which will raise your overall awareness of adversity as a simple fact of life.

Create choices. The best leaders always have at least a plan B, and often a C, D, and E to go with it. Having options is especially important during times of hardship and adversity. You can start by imagining the best possible option, but also think about outcomes that would be tolerable, at least in the short term. You are definitely going to deal with some kind of adversity during Hell Week. As you prepare, think about one possible scenario, and the various choices you'll give yourself to get out of it.

Forget excuses. If choice is the enemy of fear, as the saying goes, then excuses are one of its staunchest allies. We have a tendency to shut down and ignore our options when faced with challenging situations, and that opens the door for all kinds of excuse making. And excuses have a way of building on one another, accruing into full-fledged denial. You're faced with a problem. You come up with a list of excuses for why you can't deal with it. Eventually, you convince yourself that the problem isn't so bad, when in fact it's getting bigger all the time. During Hell Week, you will find the courage to banish excuses and confront adversity head-on.

Think about it. Overcoming adversity is a kind of problem solving, and one of the best ways to tackle a problem is to come at it with a clear mind. That involves learning how to get yourself into a calm state where you have full control over your emotions, which is another reason I'm such a big proponent of meditation. I'll come back to it many times throughout the book, but in the context of adversity, let me just say this: I've never known a committed meditator who hadn't also learned how to embrace adversity. The skills are practically one and the same.

Find the humor. We all know about the power of laughter to lift our spirits. Humor is a great antidote to all kinds of adversity. One technique that I encourage many of my clients to try, especially the hopelessly serious ones, is to skip—I mean the kind of skipping children do when they're on their way to school. You might skip down the hall or across the parking lot or, if you must, around your office with the door closed. Wherever you do it, I guarantee the act of skipping will bring a smile to your face. That brief moment of levity will empower you to embrace adversity.

DAVE'S STORY

I definitely don't do as well as I'd like with adversity. The whole "no pain, no gain" thing never really grabbed me. I've leaned toward the path of least resistance throughout much of my life. As I think about all this ahead of Hell Week, I'm not sure if it's fear or laziness that's to blame. Probably it was some combination of the two. But when I do think back over my life, there were definitely times when I embraced adversity and took on more than I thought I could handle. There were the years I lived overseas in my twenties, including a lot of lonely times. Getting a master's degree while holding down a job. Losing my mother to cancer. Working with a therapist on some personal issues. Thinking back on those experiences, which were definitely hard, I realize there's a lot I can do. So I'll keep that in mind as I hit any low points in Hell Week or after.

ADAM'S STORY

I'm kind of the king of excuses—just ask my ex-wife. So that part of the action plan jumped out at me. I've vowed to get into shape hundreds of times over the last decade, maybe more. But I always seem to come up with a good excuse to put it off. Or I'll start for a few days, only to hit on the perfect reason for giving up. It might be a conference I have to attend in a few weeks that's going to make it impossible (or so I tell myself) to work out and stick to a healthy diet. Instead of putting in a few weeks of healthy living and seeing what happens at the confer-ence, I'll write off the entire month and swear to start as soon as I get back from the trip—which, of course, doesn't happen. It's going to be tough to break out of this pattern of thinking, but I know I need to.

STEP TWO: GET MENTALLY PREPARED

There are many ways to think about mental preparation, but in my experience, it boils down to one thing: developing a tolerance for risk. I have never encountered a worthwhile choice that wasn't coupled with some element of risk. As I see it, a choice without risk is either a false choice or a choice not worth making.

Imagine you're offered your dream job, or your dream investor comes along, ready to fund your business venture. On the face of it, accepting the job or taking the money might seem like a no-brainer. But whether you realize it or not, every opportunity comes with certain risks—often critical ones.

If history has taught us anything, it is that the future is largely unpredictable. You might accept that dream job today only to lose it tomorrow. You might grow your start-up to rival Google or Facebook, and then watch it become the next Blockbuster Video. Indeed, risk is all around us.

And yet, risk assessment doesn't inform our decision to the extent that it should. When I was eighteen and invested everything I had and everything I was into becoming a paratrooper, there was no guarantee that I would get in. But I was completely dedicated to the decision. I gave it my all. Of course, so did each of the other hopefuls seeking admittance. The numbers were stacked against me. The only thing I knew for certain was that I felt good about my choice, and so I accepted the risk of failure. It is rare to change your mind when you feel good about something, no matter the risk.

As you prepare for Hell Week, I want you to remember this good feeling. We have a word for this in Norwegian: *godfølelse*. To go for *godfølelse* (gofø'ləlsə) is to create the best possible life, one that fulfills and excites you every day. When we follow that good feeling, what we are really doing is letting our emotions determine our actions. That's a positive thing, despite the bad rap emotions often get—especially in the business world, where leaders are supposed to be steely and unflappable. I take the opposite view. In my experience, life-changing decisions are always emotional reactions, and the stronger the emotion, the more confident you will feel that your decision is the right one. If all the data you can gather is telling you to change careers to a safer, more stable line of work, you won't do it if you are passionate about your current occupation.

In the last chapter, I talked about the car accident that changed my life. The words of my father and minister were instrumental in my recovery, but there was one other influence that's worth mentioning here. At the encouragement of a close friend, I traveled to England to listen to Tony Robbins, the life performance coach. (I sat on the edge of my chair for three days; the seminar was a game changer for me and motivated me to do what I do today.) Tony has many interesting and important ideas in the motivational speeches he gives, but what I respect the most about his teachings is the emphasis on emotion. "What is your motive for action? What is it that drives you in your life?" he asks. "I believe emotion is the force of life."

I couldn't agree more, and yet our culture tends to value information more highly than feelings. So even though we base most of our major choices on feelings, we like to tell ourselves that the opposite is true, that we actually base our choices mostly on information. That simply isn't the case, which is why the first step of Hell Week is about letting go of that risk-obsessed voice of reason and instead focusing on your feelings, which are what drive us into action.

Think of your own ultimate dream. You can either listen to your feelings that are screaming for you to pursue it, or you can obey the numbers that say you will never beat the odds. Risk is essentially information on possible outcomes. Whichever outcome you respond to with the most emotion is more often than not the course of action you will pursue. When you listen to your emotions and decide to go for it, you will find that no amount of information on other possible outcomes will dissuade you. Emotion is the true influencer of your decisions, not information.

It's not enough to understand rationally that being overweight is unhealthy, or that smoking can cause lung cancer. Everybody knows these things, but people go on overeating and smoking. Change is not driven by information. You can study how to become better at anything, but if you are expecting your behavior to change based on the information you garner, you will be waiting a long time.

If you study your life choices, you will come to realize that each one has been driven by an emotion. If you make up your mind to stop being overweight, the choice is driven by a desire to feel better about your body. If you decide to concentrate solely on landing the big-fish clients, it's because you are tired of being mediocre and working hard with little payoff. But there is no need to wait until you are fed up to decide to change. Through mental training, you can learn to channel your emotions today.

One of my key roles as a mental trainer is to help you use your emotions to effect change. You want to become a better version of yourself and dare to pursue your dreams. All of us do. But to do that, you have to feel strongly that you are doing the right thing. If not, you will end up focusing on the risks of change and you will find yourself becoming emotionally motivated to play it safe. You will not change. You will stay where you are.

Have you ever attended a leadership course? You leave for the course with a vision of yourself as an empowered leader with improved management skills, but when you return to the office, you are met with your old self. If the training didn't invigorate you on an emotional level, you remain the same person you were before you took the course. Nothing has changed.

If we want to become better, why do we need emotion? Why don't we just change anyway? The answer, I believe, is that humans don't actually like to change. Change is painful and it involves the unknown. It's human nature to resist change, to avoid or postpone it. The only way to create the necessary momentum to break this pattern of sameness is to appeal to your emotions.

How do I stir up the emotions of my clients? I provoke them deliberately. I get them out of the stupor of their comfort zone. Many people from the sports and business worlds have never made the decision to go all out, to truly go after their goal. They hope to reach it someday. They might even believe it will happen, but hoping and believing are no guarantees of success. They're essentially just dreaming. The power of change resides in you making up your mind to really do it—to act as though you must. There is no other way.

This is the decision I provoke in my clients. If a client reveals a motivation for achieving a goal, then we're really getting somewhere. If you can't formulate why you want to change, then your emotional attachment to your desired outcome is too weak. When you put your motivation for achieving a goal into words, you begin to realize that results will not magically materialize on their own. You are the one who has to make some changes. More important, you are coming close to realizing your emotional motivation for change.

When I work with top athletes, I often say, "If you keep doing what you have been doing, you will continue getting the same results, year after year. Best-case scenario, your career will end with a fifth ranking. Is that what you want, or are you ready to make some changes?"

To someone who wants to lose weight, I might say, "Where will you be in five years if you continue eating the same foods you are eating now? You will most likely weigh at least an extra twenty pounds. An extra twenty pounds! This means you will be less fit, less energetic, and feel even more miserable than you already are."

Here's another hard truth about human nature, in addition

to its resistance to change: most people are inherently lazy. We get in a rut and we stay there. We simply shuffle along on the track life placed us on that is most likely taking us somewhere we don't really want to go. To shake people out of the numbness of life, it helps to ask provoking questions: Do you expect something to happen on its own? Is this really what you want? Do you want to be a comfort-oriented middle manager for the rest of your career? Is this really your peak?

In addition to asking yourself the tough questions, you need to work on building up your resilience. Here are some strategies to work on before Hell Week to help build up your mental toughness.

THE ACTION PLAN

Silence the negative voices. It's easy to blame yourself for being stuck in a rut. You focus on all the wrong choices you made. Or you tell yourself that your heart has never been in it. To break this pattern of pessimism, you literally need to turn off the negative voices in your head. It requires deliberate focus and concentration. As you prepare for Hell Week, I want you to be vigilant of these negative thoughts and defuse them by making the conscious decision not to listen to them. You might even go so far as to yell the word *Stop!* in your mind. Do whatever it takes to break the negative thought cycle so that you can point your thoughts in a positive direction.

Learn to deal with discomfort. An entire day of Hell Week will be devoted to getting outside of your comfort zone. During the preparatory stage, I simply want you to imagine the feeling by asking yourself some of the same provocative questions I ask my clients. What would happen if you lost it all tomorrow? How would you respond? What would you do first? Be as realistic as possible in these doomsday scenarios. See yourself rising from bed, getting dressed, and putting your life back together. This thought experiment is designed to reveal your resilience, which in turn should instill higher levels of risk tolerance.

Embrace your silly side. I already mentioned the power of skipping, as in skipping down the street, to lighten your mood and help with relaxation. It's also a good way to get out of your comfort zone. Picture a judge skipping to the courtroom or a college president skipping across campus. Kind of unimaginable, right? Onlookers might even think they looked foolish. But what if that judge or president made it known that skipping was his or her way of destressing and that it was essential to the work they did? The action would probably then be perceived differently, as the action of an enlightened man or woman. Obviously there is a time and place for silliness—the judge wouldn't skip while court was in session, nor would the president during a commencement speech. But in the right setting, embracing your silly side is an effective way to get outside of your comfort zone.

Be okay with "I don't know." Imagine you're asked a question that you don't know the answer to. Now imagine it's a question you really should be able to answer and is being asked by someone you don't want to look stupid in front of. In that situation, most people will do their best to feign knowledge in some way, or maybe they'll try to deftly change the conversation so their ignorance isn't exposed. Admitting they don't know is too un-comfortable. But why? Is there anyone in the world who knows everything? Of course not. And even the most intelligent among us have huge gaps in their knowledge. Saying *I don't know* is a great way to get outside of your comfort zone. And I think you'll find that it leads to a lot more learning.

JILLIAN'S STORY

The words "I don't know" aren't really in my vocabulary, especially when it comes to work. And even as a kid I didn't do a lot of embracing of my silly side (not sure I even had one). At first, I didn't really get Erik's argument that these steps are part of mental preparation. I might have assumed the opposite—you know, that getting mentally prepared means adopting a serious mind-set and believing you have all the answers. But I see what he's saying. Pretending to have all the answers all the time is totally exhausting, and it's made me vulnerable in a lot of different ways. Same thing with maintaining a serious demeanor. I'm not sure I'm going to start skipping down the hallways at the office, but I will look for ways to bring a little more levity to my job and life.

DAVE'S STORY

Risk tolerance isn't exactly in my blood. When I was growing up, my father was always worried about money, despite the fact that he was a successful vice president at a big public relations firm. He had four kids to put through college and a nice house in the suburbs, so there were a lot of responsibilities. As a result, he stayed in a career that he really didn't like for thirty years. He himself had grown up in a pretty poor home, so the prospect was very real to him—the thought of losing the house or not being able to put his kids through college. I relate to that, now that I have a mortgage and mouths to feed. So getting comfortable with risk is going to be a huge challenge. But it's one I want to take. Because I look at my dad now, and I know he regrets the way his professional life played out. I don't want to go down the same path.

STEP THREE: STRENGTHEN THE CONNECTION BETWEEN MIND AND BODY

Most of us are expert excuse-makers. There is no weight-loss goal, muscle-gain regimen, or core-strengthening routine that we can't justify our way out of. We are great liars. We are even better at believing our own lies.

When it comes to physical fitness, we tend to believe our excuses for being out of shape are not just obstacles, but impassable walls. This just isn't the case. One of the reasons we never get around to actually putting on the running shoes and getting out the door is that we focus on the physical work ahead and then give up. When we do this, we are tying our laces before we put on our shoes. We are not learning to fight the mental battle before we get to the physical one. Exercise that succeeds on the track or in the gym starts in the mental ring.

What are some of the final scores in these mental matches? No time to work out? You just lost the game 0–1. You will hit the gym next week? You just upped your losing streak to two. Too tired? You forfeit the match.

The important thing to understand is that losing the physical fitness game means losing the mental edge that will get you ahead in the professional world. The discipline and mental clarity that comes from keeping your body in shape cannot be gained any other way than through regular exercise.

The athlete is the perfect example of someone who unites the physical and mental into one. Athletes understand that the performance of the body and mind are linked, and that neglecting one will adversely affect the performance of the other. Athletes constantly combat the thoughts that are begging them to quit the painful climb to reach peak condition. They cannot succeed physically if they are not mentally tough. Athletes know that the body and the mind complement each other when trained well. They depend on it.

You might think that this kind of mind-and-body unity is a benefit enjoyed only by professional athletes, who have nothing but their physical conditioning to be concerned with. Not true. We can gain the same mental benefits from physical exercise that athletes do. Do not let yourself think athletes are some other type of human born for exercise. They weren't born that way any more than CEOs were born with an executive gene.

The athlete is no superhuman, but the best ones carefully use mental focus to increase physical output. The opposite works just as well. You can use physical activity to increase mental strength. You are the product of physical behavior that has real mental outcomes. In your profession, I'm sure you have seen some succeed while others have failed, in the same way most athletes remain average while others excel. The difference between an average athlete and an excellent athlete is that the excellent athlete performs every day. The same is true for you. You cannot win on game day if you don't win the other days as well.

Yes, you will sometimes lose. No matter how hard you work, you will sometimes fail. Even the most focused athlete cannot exceed his or her own potential. Some will train their whole lives and never break a record or win a gold medal. You are not in control of everything in your life, nor will you ever be. Recognizing this is a key step in getting mentally in shape. But an even more important key is knowing that while you can never control every variable, you can control your mind to stay committed to exercise. If you learn to do this, there will be few professional goals outside your reach.

Let's look at an example of how body and mind interact. Try to remember one of your worst days at work. You felt like garbage and so you performed like it. You avoided looking people in the eye, maybe even staring at the floor on your way to and from lunch. In a meeting you wasted numerous chances to make yourself known. At one point during the day, you gave up completely and whittled away an hour by surfing the Internet. When it came time to go home, you realized the day was a complete waste. Whatever you did accomplish was half-baked and you took forever getting it done at all.

Now ask yourself, has it ever been impossible, except in the most tragic of circumstances, to consciously change your mood? Is it impossible to change your worst day into a passable or even great day? The answer is almost too obvious. You are in control of your mind, and with that control you are in charge of your mood. You decide how your day is.

What if you had begun that day with a vigorous run? Like all exercise, running has an instant positive effect on your mind and mood. Think of the times when you have felt a little down, tired, or insecure, and then have forced yourself to exercise, despite being incredibly unmotivated. After only a few minutes, you start to feel more positive, energized, and clearheaded. Afterward, when you're in the shower, your feelings and mind-set are totally different from when you started your run. You have used your mental strength to exercise, and your exercise has altered your mental state. If you wake up with the feeling that today is going to be an off day, exercise. It will change you.

President Barack Obama once said that when he has to choose between sleeping an extra hour and going for a run, he always chooses to run. "I get positive, clearheaded, and find solutions when I run," he says.

Physical fitness even influences body language. Studies show that if you're slouching in your chair, you are less receptive to new knowledge than if you were sitting with a straight back while leaning forward. If you hold a pen between your fingers and lay your hands on the desk, the effect will be even stronger. The way in which you use your body sends signals to your brain. When your body is alert, the mind cannot simultaneously be slouching and sagging. If you sit upright and lean forward, a posture that indicates attentiveness, your body will signal your brain to pay attention because something important is going on.

If you shuffle around with short, hasty steps right before an important meeting or a competition, you will automatically become more nervous. Behaving nervously makes you nervous. Throughout the years, your brain has been taught to equate these exact motions with nervousness. But you don't want to be nervous, and you can replace this feeling with something else. Starting with your body language may be a smart thing to do.

When I struggled during the last day of Hell Week for paratrooper admission trials, I forced a smile on my face. The brain associates the muscles used for smiling with something positive, and in a flash, you will feel a little lighter. You can try it next time you wake up feeling really exhausted.

Forcing yourself to breathe calmly and with your stomach can make you a little bit calmer, and this may be what it takes to do a good job. Your brain associates calm and deep breathing with relaxation. Breathe in deeply, and breathe out slowly. The importance of breathing is also recognized in the martial arts, yoga, and the military. Controlling your breath can determine how you feel. A Navy SEAL told me they use a technique where they divide the inhalation into three stages: halfway in, a quarter in, another quarter in. They breathe in through the mouth, inhaling 50 percent. They stop for a second, draw the breath farther down the lungs another 25 percent, stop for a second, and then breathe in the remaining 25 percent, finally exhaling slowly through the nose. The purpose is to shift the focus from chaos to calm, from the external (the act of shooting) to the internal (breathing).

The SEALs rehearse it again and again during training with a lot of emphasis ("Mind your breathing! In-in-in!"). After a while, calm settles in. If you only focus on the danger, on the external threat, you forget that you can actually use this technique to take optimal action. If you are being shot at, it's natural to be stressed and scared, and to hyperventilate. A soldier cannot always change his circumstances, but he can do something to alter his own attitude. That's why he starts to focus on his breathing. This will lead the soldier to move his focus from the danger of being shot at to automatically doing the things he has rehearsed: placing the gunstock on the shoulder, his right hand on the grip, and pulling the trigger. What the Navy SEALs hope to achieve with this breathing technique is to enter into the necessary mental state to solve the physical situation.

But how do stress and other anxiety-producing emotions arise in the first place? The answer is not as obvious as you might think. The American psychologist and philosopher William James has argued in his now-famous theory that we don't run away from a bear because we're afraid of it, but rather the other way around: we are afraid because we run away from the bear. It's not actually as strange as it may sound, and James's theory has since found a lot of support from the field of modern neurological science. James wanted to find out about the relation between cause and effect when it comes to human emotions. Does the external factor (the bear) cause the emotion (fear), and then the ensuing reaction (running away)? Or does the reaction (running away) create the emotion (fear)?

According to James's theory, emotion is caused by a series of events beginning with a stimulus in the nervous system, before its manifestation as a conscious experience (joy, anger, fear, etc.). This led James to ask himself the question about the bear. Because emotions are almost always accompanied by bodily reactions (heart pounding, hands sweating, etc.), couldn't it just as well be that this bodily reaction is the cause of the emotion, and not the other way around? We think that we cry because we are sad, but couldn't it be that we are sad because we are crying? Or, at least, that these two factors are working together?

James's theories are still subject to a lot of research. What's interesting in this context, though, is the idea that bodily reactions are able to cause emotions, or at least that the body and emotions can amplify one another. Bearing this in mind, you will also be able to exploit it and thus be able to manipulate the way you feel.

A downcast gaze is a prime example of feelings of inferiority. A deep voice is perceived as more assuring and more authoritative than a higher one. If you know the first sentence in your speech or presentation by heart, and you are able to deliver it in a deep, controlled voice while holding a steady gaze and a good posture, it will immediately reduce any feelings of tension you may have to begin with.

The same thing can be said about the clothes you wear. If you feel attractive, it will influence your posture and your entire attitude. If you are conscious of this, you can dress the way you would like to feel.

Attention to detail is important in achieving a successful mind-set. The Special Forces take this to the extreme, because they know that details can be the difference between survival and death. It's the same with sports and business. The details decide the difference between the best and the second best. It's not a coincidence that antiterror units all over the world dress in black. It's not only for tactical reasons—it also looks tough. It's a lot more frightening when someone comes at you dressed all in black than in shocking pink. They dress with courage and an aggressive attitude.

Put another way, using a refrain you often hear in sports, "Look good, feel good, play good." If you're in the best shape of your life, and you're putting great food into your body, and you're getting the rest you need, and you're impeccably dressed—if you do all these things, I promise you that the positive results will follow from your mental state. Here are the specific steps to get you there.

THE ACTION PLAN

Exercise every day. You must work out for a minimum of one hour each day during Hell Week. At least two of these exercise sessions should be extremely vigorous, enough to cause sweat and heavy breathing. If you aren't regularly active, you should get clearance from your doctor before taking on this rigorous regimen. It's a good idea to ask them what a safe heart rate is for your condition and then use a heart-rate monitor to make sure you're staying within it.

Increase your activity. In addition to regular exercise, you should lead an overall more active life during Hell Week. If possible, walk or ride your bike to work, instead of driving or relying on mass transportation. Walk briskly or even take a light jog between meetings or when going for a cup of coffee.

Master your mode. Mode is a state that allows you to trust your training and to act in the way you do in training—to act instinctively. If you are in danger, it is natural to feel scared, maybe even to panic. But that feeling is not going to make you safe from what you fear. You therefore need to override the natural feeling and change it into another. Below is the advice I give corporate managers who are about to deliver important presentations, or to artists who are about to go onstage. As part of your Hell Week preparation, practice these techniques so that you can implement them when the main event arrives.

- Breathe deeply and feel calmer.
- Square your shoulders. You will feel a little safer.
- Walk at a brisk, confident stride, and you will feel more sure of yourself.
- Smile to feel more positive and happier.
- Sit or stand with your body leaning forward to feel more alert.
- Stand with your feet set wide apart to feel tougher and more powerful.

Eat well. A healthy diet is essential to peak performance. Before the start of Hell Week, stock up on healthy foods, including fruits and vegetables, nuts and whole grains, and yogurt. You should eat smaller meals more frequently throughout the day, preferably five small meals a day, two of which should be snacks. Forget the junk food and forgo alcohol. You won't have to deny yourself these indulgences forever, but during Hell Week only the best food and drink should enter your body.

Dress for success. I'm not what you'd call a clotheshorse, but I still wear a suit to work almost every day. I can feel my mind-set start to shift as I put on my executive uniform. It has an effect on me: shaving thoroughly, putting on a freshly ironed shirt, bending the collar of my shirt over the tie, or fine-tuning the crease in my pants. I want you to prepare for this kind of personal presentation before Hell Week. When you dress professionally, it doesn't feel natural to surf the web and gossip with coworkers. Smart attire is a reminder that you're in work mode. It communicates to colleagues, clients, and yourself that you're someone who pays attention to detail, to doing things properly, and that you're reliable.

Adam's Story

I was actually a very serious athlete growing up—a three-sport varsity athlete in high school, back when kids played more than one sport. I took up rugby in college, and that kept me involved in competitive sports into my mid-twenties. But then I just got too busy to make the commitment, and without the structure of a team and a schedule and all that, I basically stopped exercising completely. I always assumed I'd find some other outlet, like jogging or joining the gym. But I never developed the discipline to self-motivate. It's like I needed a coach blowing the whistle or team captain shouting orders—otherwise I wasn't getting off the couch. I still run into old teammates and they always do a double take at how soft I've become. You'd think it would motivate me to want to change, but that hasn't been the case so far.

Dave's Story

I've played sports my entire life, mostly soccer and tennis, and I'm a pretty avid runner. There's a gym at work and I get to it a few days a week. So on the surface I have a pretty active, fit lifestyle. But I don't go nearly as hard as I could or should. Ever since turning forty, I've had a harder time keeping off the weight (for the first time ever, there was a two at the start of my weight when I stepped on the scale a few weeks back!). And I've definitely lost a few steps on the soccer field, where a lot of the guys are in their twenties and thirties. Basically, I need to step it up.

As I came to that realization in the context of Hell Week preparation, I realized that I've never been 100 percent committed to being in peak physical shape. Even in college, when I played Division 1 soccer, I was part of the crew that partied hard after the games and lived on pizza and fast food. Not surprisingly, I never made it onto the starting eleven, and by senior year I'd quit the team completely. I wonder what kind of playing career I would have had if I'd been more committed.

I can't turn back the clock, but I'm hoping Hell Week will motivate me to take my workouts more seriously. I'd love to lose the "dad bod" and look as good as possible. Obviously diet plays a part in that, too. I've definitely developed some bad habits over the years—some of which go all the way back to those raucous college years. It's definitely time to rethink the way I treat my body.

STEP FOUR: GATHER FEEDBACK

This is one step where the professional athletes I've worked with have a clear advantage, since their performances are usually played out under the microscope. They're filmed, observed, and critiqued every day, whether during training sessions or live competition. I remember working with the Norwegian cross-country team during a training camp in Italy. These guys were getting it from every angle—their coaches and teammates, the public and the press. Everywhere they turned, there was someone new with words of wisdom on how to improve their technique or shave another quarter second off their split times.

Granted, that kind of intense and incessant feedback presents its own challenges. But it's fair to say that the typical professional athlete has a pretty clear idea about his or her strengths and weaknesses. It's not so easy for the rest of us. As a result, we have a tendency to hide behind PowerPoint presentations or prestigious corporate logos, rather than looking fear in the eye and really taking the time to understand how the rest of the world perceives us.

That's what the gathering-feedback step is all about. Over the course of several weeks, I want you to reach out to people from your professional and personal lives and ask them what they really think about your actions, your attitudes, and your performances. It's fine to include your closest friend from the office in the evaluations, but in order to get the richest possible feedback, try also to speak to people with whom you don't already have a strong personal connection. Remember, you want to know how you come across in meetings with that first-time client or new office colleague. For that, you need to hear from people who don't know everything about you. Their feedback won't be as personally probing as what you hear from friends and family members, but that's okay. The goal here is to get a complete picture of how you're seen by other people, even at an objective first-impression level.

Especially when they come from the business world, clients I work with often have no idea what their coworkers really think of them. That's a problem, since perception counts for so much in the workplace. There was the executive at a global consulting firm who worked incredibly hard, from early morning to late at night, and demanded the same of his staff. His work ethic was driven by passion and a desire for his team and his company to succeed. Unfortunately, his reputation for being something of a tyrant got in the way of those goals, since people didn't want to work for him, and those who did suffered from low morale.

His example reminded me of the maxim in sports—whether soccer, baseball, basketball, or some other game—which says that great players don't necessarily make great coaches. The reason is that they can't understand why their players can't play the same way they did. They chalk it up to laziness or lack of discipline or some other deficiency, when in fact many of their players simply don't have the same abilities. It's not that they're talentless, and they may actually be better in some aspects of the game. But the coach, because he hasn't learned the difference between playing and teaching, can't separate their strengths from his own weaknesses.

I had another client, this one an executive at a technology firm, who had the opposite problem. He had difficulty promoting himself and his accomplishments because he worried it would come across as too self-aggrandizing and that his team would think he was taking all the credit for the work they did together.

Gender can play a huge role in workplace perception, more so for women in my experience, who often have to contend with gender-based stereotyping—for example, the one that posits that women are best at "taking care," while men are best at "taking charge." In reality, of course, men and women are equally capable in both departments. But I've worked with many women who worry that colleagues will perceive their can-do, problem-solving attitude as being overly aggressive.

Dealing with stereotypes is one thing, but before you can get there, you need to understand how others really and truly see you. A lot of people are isolated in their leadership roles. Let's face it: being in charge requires a certain measure of detachment. The boss might be able to join the team for drinks every now and then, but if he or she is trying to tag along every Friday night, overfamiliarity, a lack of boundaries, and a loss of respect are sure to ensue.

I've found that the best leaders often have a person from

outside the company or corporation with whom they can vent their frustrations or debate difficult questions. The sounding board/sparring partner could be a friend, a former coworker, a mentor, or a mental trainer like myself.

The point is that they are continually getting feedback on their ideas and their actions. Without this, I find that leaders don't develop the ability to adapt their behavior to different people in different situations. Instead, they behave the same way toward everyone, regardless of the circumstances. Think of the image of the high-powered executive barking orders at his kids' Little League team.

Leaders must be able to adjust—or "pivot," to use the term of the moment. They must be able to read people. They must be willing to expand their repertoire of management techniques. Without fail, leaders who are able to employ a wide range of management techniques throughout their workweek achieve the best results. Leaders who identify these skills and practice them are more likely to succeed than those who seldom think about their own development.

That's what the feedback phase is all about. Through structured conversations with people in your life, you will get a clear idea of how you're perceived in the real world. You will be able to list your strengths and weaknesses. Once you have the information, you will then be able to develop a strategy for putting forward your best possible self. I'll give you an example of how this works.

Megan was a middle manager at a production company who knew from the feedback she'd received that she needed to be more assertive. In her mind, she always thought she was encouraging her employees by creating an open work environment where ideas were welcome. But after soliciting feedback, she realized that the signal she was sending was one of indecisiveness.

During one of our first sessions, we talked about small steps she could take to change that perception. We decided, for instance, that Megan would talk a little more loudly during her next staff meeting. She would also use more decisive body language—for example, leaning in toward each person as they spoke. Those simple steps helped her feel more assertive and, in turn, self-confident.

With that experience behind her, Megan imagined herself being even more direct before her next meeting (I'll discuss this technique, called visualization, in more detail in a later phase of Hell Week preparation). Ahead of her third meeting, we planned for her to propose an idea that she knew several team members would oppose. She prepared for the pushback by coming up with solid answers to their criticism and skepticism that she delivered firmly but fairly. Indeed, "firm but fair" became a personal mantra that she repeated before meetings.

Additionally, Megan started telling herself on a daily basis, "You are an assertive, tough, straightforward, and confident leader with a capital L." She used an image—the insignia from her college, where she was a standout volleyball player—that symbolized this new personality as the wallpaper on her phone. We continued to talk about other situations where she would have an opportunity to exercise assertiveness. Slowly but surely, a new and vastly improved Megan emerged. To her surprise and delight, her colleagues weren't put off in the least by her new attitude. To the contrary, they worked harder for her and with her than ever before, and within a year Megan was promoted to senior management.

Megan made all the right moves to change her career and take it to the next level. It took a lot of effort and discipline. But first she had to identify the problem, which she did by gathering feedback from the people around her. You need to do the same. Here's how:

THE ACTION PLAN

Draw from all spheres of your life. There's no single right number for how many people you should interview, but I do want the feedback to come from all aspects of your life. Remember, we all have different personas—one for work, one for family, one for friends, etc. I think you'll find that some of the qualities you hear about from your home life might be applicable to work. Or if you're in a book club or on a hockey team, the feedback you receive about the person you are in that setting could be applied during your next sales pitch or job interview.

Give people time to prepare. Stopping a colleague in the hallway at work and asking them what they think about you will probably put them on the spot. Likewise, you don't want to ambush a friend during an otherwise casual drink at the bar. I tell my clients to be clear and up-front about Hell Week and the role feedback plays in the process. The other people are usually intrigued and eager to participate (indeed, more than a few have turned into clients themselves). It helps to set a date at least forty-eight hours in advance so that your interviewees will have time to think about the feedback they're going to give. And it helps to give them a few questions to ponder. The questions should be specific and pointed. Instead of "What are my strengths and weaknesses?" you might ask, "Are there ways that I could run our weekly meetings more effectively?" or "Do I provide adequate direction when assigning you projects?"

Listen up. This should be obvious, but if you're a person who is used to doing most of the talking (and many of my clients do fall into that category), you need to remind yourself that this is a time to open your ears and keep your mouth shut. You may not agree with every point your interviewee makes—and some of them might make you downright angry—but the goal of this exercise is to understand how others perceive you, and not how you think you should be perceived. Engage in active listening through maintained eye contact, small smiles, and attentive posture.

Include written responses. Even with ample warning, some people won't be comfortable giving you feedback in person. It's okay to include some written exchanges in the process. I don't like clients to rely on the written word completely, since face-to-face interactions tend to contain the emotion that's key to the process. But one or two written responses can help bring in different perspectives.

Try for some anonymous response. This is a little harder to pull off, but if you can find a way to solicit anonymous feedback, it's guaranteed to be honest (though be warned, the truth can sting!). When I'm working with clients, I'll often orchestrate interviews with coworkers, which is one way of achieving anonymity. You won't have that same luxury, but you might enlist a spouse, partner, or close colleague to get some anonymous feedback on your behalf.

Forget the performance appraisal. This might not win me many friends in human resources departments, but the once- or twice-a-year performance review doesn't help employees really reach their full potential. Sure, it serves some purpose, giving managers and employees alike a chance to assess accomplishments and set goals for the coming year. But the entire process is too formal and regimented. The kind of feedback I want you to get for Hell Week needs a stronger emotional core. This is more likely to happen when you initiate the conversation outside of the appraisal process. I had one client who started going on power walks at lunch with her colleagues, and those walks led to some of their most meaningful exchanges. Look for that kind of fresh, unexpected context.

Make room for follow-ups. If you end up having a lively and productive discussion or written exchange with your interviewee, chances are additional thoughts will occur to them later on. Let them know that they're welcome to share anything else that comes to mind at any time. Also, you might offer to give them feedback on their performance, if it seems like they'd be amenable. More companies are making this process formal through so-called "360-degree reviews." I see a lot of value in this approach, though you don't have to wait for it to become official policy at your job. Being able to offer criticism is just as valuable as being able to receive it—and this phase of Hell Week preparation is a perfect forum for that sort of give-and-take.

DAVE'S STORY

I'm not a very confrontational person by nature, so this was a difficult exercise. I felt like I'd be putting people on the spot or in an uncomfortable position. I decided to approach a colleague from work who I have lunch with every couple weeks. He's in a different department, but we work on a few projects a year, so I thought he'd have a pretty good perspective. He made two points, both of which kind of surprised me. First, he said that other people in the company, especially new hires, often assume I'm the head of my department. He thought it had to do with the way I dress and carry myself, but also my manner in meetings. I felt good about that. His second point wasn't as positive. He basically said that I could also be a little intimidating at times. That really floored me, because in my mind I'm often doubting myself and carrying around a lot of insecurities. But the feelings are clearly coming across differently.

This was helpful feedback. The fact that people view me as a leader is encouraging. I need to own that more and use it to my advantage. But I also need to recognize that my insecurities can translate into a kind of aggression. I know that I tend to get quiet when I'm feeling unsure, and maybe that silence comes across as judgmental. During Hell Week, I'm going to look out for this, and work extra hard at projecting openness, even when I'm feeling unsure on the inside.

JILLIAN'S STORY

This was super-uncomfortable, because I'm not someone who does a lot of opening up with people. Maybe it's the English blood in me. So I actually avoided even thinking about it for a few weeks. But then I finally bit the bullet and had a chat with one of my colleagues from the office, a woman I've known for a bunch of years. We actually worked together at another bank before our current job, which is something she talked about. We'd been in more junior positions back then, and she talked about how much more relaxed I was in that job. I felt myself becoming defensive. I wanted to explain that I have more re-sponsibility now and that's stressful, so of course I'm not going to be as much fun. But as I thought about it more, I realized that she was right—I was more relaxed in my last job, and as a result I was a lot better in that role as well. The ultra-serious approach I'm taking with my current position isn't necessarily leading to better results.

STEP FIVE: DEFINE YOUR GOALS

My job as a mental trainer would not be possible without the notion of goals. The ability to set and achieve new goals, as much as opposable thumbs and upright posture, is what makes us human. Of course, some of us do a better job than others. That's what we'll focus on in this stage of your Hell Week preparation—learning how to create goals that are rooted in your value system and aimed at your highest levels of need.

To begin, let me share one of my favorite lessons from philosophy class.

The professor stood before his students with various objects on the desk in front of him. Without saying a word, he lifted up a large, empty mayonnaise jar and filled it to the brim with golf balls.

"Is the jar full?" he asked. The class answered yes.

Next, the professor lifted a canister containing pebbles and poured them into the mayonnaise jar. He shook the jar lightly, and the pebbles rolled down into the spaces between the golf balls.

Again he asked if the jar was now full. Again, his students replied that it was.

The professor picked up a container of sand and poured it into the jar. The grains of sand filled the remaining spaces in the jar. He asked if the jar was now full, and the students gave an unequivocal yes.

The professor now fetched a large cup of coffee from underneath the desk and poured the contents into the jar with the sand. The coffee filled the spaces around the grains of sand. The students laughed.

"Now," said the professor, "I want you to consider that this jar represents your life. The golf balls are the important things—family, friends, health, your greatest passions—all the things that, even if you lost everything else, would nevertheless make life worthwhile. The pebbles represent all the other things that mean something in life—your job, your house, your car. The sand is everything else—the favorite pair of shoes, the TV show you love to watch on Sunday night."

The professor went on: "If you pour the sand into the jar first, you will not have room for the pebbles and the golf balls. That's how it is in life as well. If you spend all your time and energy on the small stuff, you will never have time for the things that are really meaningful to you. So pay attention to the things that are essential for your own happiness. Play with your children. Attend your regular health checkups. Take your spouse to a romantic dinner. You will always have time to buy new clothes or watch TV. Be clear about your priorities, because all the rest is only sand."

One of the students put up his hand and asked what the coffee represented. The professor smiled. "I'm glad you asked that question," he said. "It shows quite clearly that no matter how crowded and hectic your life appears, there is always room for a cup of coffee with a friend."

I love this story because the mayonnaise jar captures the incredibly multifaceted nature of modern life, with all its golf balls, pebbles, and grains of sand. And it points to the imperative for priorities. If you don't devise a strategy for organizing your goals, you will almost certainly run into a state of paralysis. This is such a common human condition. Despite our innate capacity for change and self-improvement, all too often we don't realize what's possible because we're frozen with fear and indecision. The only way to break out of this is to think long and hard about the aspects of your life that matter most, and separate out the distractions. This is very active thinking that I'm asking you to do—whatever you need to do to access that level of deep, meditative concentration. Some people actually meditate, while others go for long walks or sit down at a café with a pen and pad. There's no right or wrong method, but you do have to commit.

I often talk of the process in terms of "cracking your code" with my clients. I get them to conduct a self-assessment to increase their self-awareness and determine where they are in relation to where they want to be in life. Many of them haven't taken a step back from their lives in years, if not decades, so the process enables them to put their lives into perspective in surprisingly quick fashion.

From there they can start to draw a map of their life, identifying goals that intersect with their true values. Consider the CEOs who lament not spending enough time with their children. Walking away from their company and their career probably isn't an option (though I suppose it does happen on occasion). That leaves them with two basic options: either they learn methods for coping with their guilty conscience or they develop strategies for setting aside more time for their family.

It's important to think both short and long term. Tennis great Andre Agassi said he never thought of grand slams or his next big match when he woke up in the morning. What he thought instead was, *When I go to bed in the evening, I am going to be proud of myself.* He was—and still is, I'm sure—conscious of this every day, and as a result he's someone who always goes to bed, if not happy, at least satisfied. And of course he's had his share of victories throughout his storied career.

The novelist Lars Saabye Christensen talks similarly about his writing process. When you're in the thick of a big, complex novel, he says, it's no use thinking of the whole of the novel each time you sit down to write: "It's not feasible, neither physically nor mentally. That's why I always set up small goals for myself. I don't think to myself that I'll sit here for three years and write four hundred pages. I would be paralyzed. But I tell myself, now my main character is getting up, and I have to pick out clothes for him, then he will descend the stairs and walk out into the street, maybe he meets someone there." Completing the novel is the ultimate goal, but along the way he sets smaller benchmarks.

Make your goal as concise and concrete as possible. I had a client, a high-powered lawyer in his midforties with a beautiful family—the kind of guy who seems to have it all. And yet, something was missing. I started our first session by asking him the usual questions about his life. There really wasn't anything wrong that he could point to, just a general malaise that so many of us experience.

Then I asked him to tell me about the last time he could remember being truly happy. He thought for a few seconds and then told me that he was last happy when he was first starting out at the law firm where he was now partner.

"How would you describe your life at that time?" I asked him.

He talked about the long hours and the difficulty of absorbing so much new information and other stuff that didn't actually sound so pleasant. I pointed this out to him. "Yeah, but it was great being in the trenches with the other associates," he said. "Plus I had such a clear goal," he added, almost as an afterthought.

"Exactly," I said. He looked at me and the lightbulb went off, and we went on to work together on creating a new set of goals for him to work toward, using the techniques that follow.

THE ACTION PLAN

Be as specific as possible. It's one thing to say you want to make a lot of money. It's another to say you want to be worth X million dollars by the time you reach a certain age. The more specific the goal, the more likely you are to reach it, because you'll be able to formulate a concrete strategy. To use a simpler example than making a lot of money—which usually requires years of effort—let's take the example of physical fitness. Declaring that you want to get in shape is unlikely to yield meaningful results. But if you say you want in six months to lose twenty pounds or run a 10K race, you'll be able to create a plan for hitting those targets. It's always a good idea to put your goals in writing so they become a kind of contract with yourself.

Dare to dream. In due course, it's important that your goals feel realistic, that they're actually within the limits of your capabilities. But to start off, I don't want you to worry too much about this, because you may not actually be the best judge of what's possible. I see this with people all the time. They set their sights too low, either because they lack confidence or because they haven't taken the time to truly investigate all the possibilities available to them. As we work through the process, goals that they thought were well beyond their reach start to seem attainable. Don't be afraid to think big in the beginning.

Create a time frame. Goals should always be grounded in some kind of time frame. Otherwise, there won't be any sense of urgency or accountability, and you'll find that weeks or months slip by without any action. To use the fitness example, if you give yourself six months to lose those twenty pounds, you'll be able to monitor your progress and reinforce the goal with each pound you shed.

Break it up. It's important to create concrete criteria for measuring progress toward your goal. Think of the football players moving down the field toward the end zone. With every first down they reach, the chains move forward, and their confidence builds. Building subtargets into your goal will make it seem more attainable and provide that sense of forward progress.

I once worked with a sales executive who wanted to start

a business and be his own boss. But he had a wife and kids, a mortgage and car payments—all the usual trappings—so the prospect of quitting his stable, well-paying, benefits-rich job was more than he could stomach. Instead of his taking that one giant step, we worked out a strategy where he would first launch a smaller version of the business on the side, while still holding down his current job. That enabled him to take small steps toward the goal—launching the website, coming up with a marketing plan, building a customer base, etc. Slowly but surely, the side business grew until it could support him and his family, at which point it became his full-time occupation. Today it's a thriving business and he's achieved his goal of self-employment. But he never would have gotten there if he hadn't broken the goal into bite-sized chunks.

Share your vision. This isn't the first time in this book that I advocate sharing, and it won't be the last either. Very few people can live their best possible life in a vacuum. And I assure you that no one ever completed Hell Week, be it the military or civilian version, by themselves. When it comes to goals, making yourself accountable to colleagues, family, or friends is a great motivator. As you reach subtargets, they'll cheer you along, and if you experience setbacks, they'll be there to provide encouragement or that much-needed shot in the arm.

Be willing to sacrifice. A truly worthy goal will compel you to give something up. You have to be willing to accept the consequences. If you want to become a leader in your field, the time and energy needed to achieve that goal are going to have to come from some other aspect of your life. This process turns into a kind of virtuous cycle. The more sacrifices you make and the more of yourself you invest, the more motivation you feel to reach the next milestone toward your ultimate goal.

Stay the course. Ultimately, you are the only person who can make your goals happen. There will be setbacks and bumps in the road. Remember to embrace adversity and recognize that it is part of the larger journey. More than talent or intelligence or people skills, your willingness to persevere will determine whether you reach your goals or not.

In addition to staying the course, you need to go all out, from start to finish. This is a tall order for people, and not just because of the discipline required. There's also the fear that if you give all of yourself and come up short, you're left with nothing. Athletes make this mistake all the time. They give only 80 or 90 percent, so that if they do lose, they can tell themselves, "Well, I didn't go all out." Don't make this mistake. Even if you don't meet your goal, as long as you gave everything you had to give, you will have reached a new milestone in your journey.

DAVE'S STORY

For me, Hell Week is all about my career. I feel like I've got the social sphere under control. Actually, I wish I could be as in charge of my career as I am of my family. But for whatever reason, being the authority figure I am as a dad doesn't translate to work. It's not that I'm this totalitarian at home and a wet noodle in the office, but I definitely have a stronger sense of self in the home sphere. This is one of the main reasons I believe I'd be an effective leader. But I need to convince the higher-ups of that. I know it's not going to happen in a single week, but I'm looking forward to showing in that time the type of leader I can be. We'll see how it goes.

ADAM'S STORY

My primary goal is to lose the weight, obviously. But I think I need to fixate less on this one objective. I get what Erik is saying, that goals need to be specific and you need to give yourself a specific time frame. So I have those specific goals in the back of my mind. There's more to this than getting back down below 200 pounds, though. I want to go back to the guy I was before I packed on the extra pounds. If I'm going to dare to dream, that's really what I'm trying to achieve. I know you can't turn back time, but I'd like to return to that earlier mind-set.

STEP SIX: VISUALIZATION— CREATING A LOOP IN THE THREAD

Visualization is a vital tool, yet too few of us use it. In the United States, sports psychologists started using visualization deliberately as early as the 1960s. Recently it has spread to Norway as well. The Norwegian Olympic team even sent four mental trainers to the 2008 Olympic games in Beijing. Yet while the power of visualization has found a solid footing among athletes, the business world hasn't quite opened its eyes to its enormous potential.

Since visualization has its strongest support among athletics, let's begin there. Standing on top of a mountain before a competition, downhill skiers visualize the route they are about to descend. You've probably seen how they close their eyes, crouch, and make small imitative movements. In their mind, they are already on the course, executing turns, negotiating difficult sections, crossing the finish line.

In one well-known sports visualization experiment, test subjects were divided into three groups: The first group did not practice basketball. The second practiced free throws on a daily basis. The third group did not practice basketball, but visualized performing the same act of throwing the ball through the hoop. After three months, those who didn't practice had not improved their scores. Those who practiced on a daily basis improved their rate of scoring by 36 percent. Those who had only visualized throwing the ball and hitting the net saw an improvement of 18 percent. If you can learn just by visualizing, imagine the edge you can have when you walk into a situation you have never been in, but have mentally visited time and time again.

For an athlete participating in the Olympics without visualization training, the sheer size of the event can cloud perception of the task ahead. For the unprepared athlete, the Olympics are overwhelming and can easily make you forget that what you are about to do is actually quite simple. Nobody gets to the Olympics without going through the motions of their discipline countless times in training, but when your eyes see the huge stadium and the roaring crowds, nothing feels familiar. You don't need to be an Olympian to know this experience well. You have experienced it speaking in a boardroom, interviewing for your dream job, starting your own company, or almost any other situation where you find yourself performing less than your best.

Visualization is the bridge that takes your practice from the gym and brings it to game day. When you use visualization, you anticipate the details of the future. If you were visualizing for a job interview, you wouldn't just imagine the interviewer shaking your hand and saying congratulations, but also what the room might look like, how you won't fiddle with your hands or look away, how you will word things, what questions you will ask, right down to what pen the interviewer might be jotting notes down with. When you get to the actual job interview, you are already familiar with your emotions, even if the specific details don't match exactly (e.g., the interviewer is a woman in a dress with a blue pen instead of the man in a sweater with a black pen that you'd imagined). You are prepared for what is coming next. You are in control of the situation, not the other way around.

When the visiting team is walking from the locker room into the home stadium of the Liverpool Football Club, at the exact point in the tunnel where the players start to hear the roar of the fans and the chanting of the Liverpool supporters, they see a sign that reads "This Is Anfield." Walking onto that field, the visiting team can't help but feel intimidated by that sign, placed there by legendary manager Bill Shankly.

Shankly was concerned with the mental side of soccer already in the 1960s, and was famous for psyching out his opponents. He made the decision for Liverpool to play in red shirts to intimidate other teams. Placement of the "This Is Anfield" sign served the same purpose. It was to remind the players of the visiting team that the match they were about to play was no regular match; it was a meeting with the famous Liverpool team, at the famous Anfield stadium.

The mental game isn't a superpower that only some of us have, though. A visiting team can just as easily turn it to their advantage if they prepare with visualization as well. Before the 2011 Nordic World ski championship, I told the men's ski team: "When you arrive at the arena, you don't want your pulse to rise dramatically just because it's a world championship and a hundred thousand live spectators are watching, as well as countless television viewers. By the time you get to the arena, you should have been there so many times in your head that you almost think of it as a regular day at work."

I did my utmost to optimize their visualization by joining

them at the hotel where they stayed for a couple of weeks before the competition. I asked them to recline in their rooms, and I asked each of them: "Today is the fifteen-kilometer classic—how do you want to feel now?"

"Calm and relaxed," they answered.

We went down to the breakfast room, and I asked them what they would feel if the weather was bad. "It doesn't matter," they said.

"What if the weather is good?"

"Doesn't matter."

"What will you see in the breakfast room? Here is the food, and over there are the athletes. There are the Swedes, and the Russians are over there. Do you recognize them?"

"Yes, many of them."

"And there you see the other Norwegians—how do you want to feel now?"

"Still cool and relaxed." Mentally, I took them to the day of the race. I told them we were in the bus on the way to the stadium.

"What do you see here?" I asked.

"Flags and people, lots of people with faces painted for the game." Mentally, we walked down to the bottom of the ski jump facility and up again where the people kept flowing in. We walked behind the ski jump. We looked at the press, the cameras, and a sea of spectators.

"How are you feeling now?"

"Still cool and relaxed."

On the day of the competition, the ski team had practiced visualization so much that they managed to stay relaxed, despite all the cameras and crowds. Mentally, they had stood on the start line many times already by the time the first starting signal sounded. The exercise I did with the men on the ski team before the world championship was a reinforced visualization. In addition to helping them picture it in their mind's eye, we physically visited each location—the hotel, the arena, imagining the paint on the faces of the spectators and pretending to hear the noise.

I have great faith in visualization. I have seen it change performance and even entire careers whenever it is applied. I have seen it work as effectively in business life as in professional sports and athletics. A business leader can mentally prepare for a pivotal negotiation meeting just the same as an athlete can imagine a completely normal day of training on game day. You can visualize your success and then actually succeed. If you can see it, you can do it.

THE ACTION PLAN

Fake it till you make it. I once had a client who was a successful businessman in mergers and acquisitions. He suffered bouts of extreme anxiety before pitch meetings with new clients, to the point where it was affecting his job performance and taking a toll on his family. One of the techniques I had him do was to tell himself every day that he was looking forward to the next pitch meeting. Even though it was patently false, repeating the statement over and over, for up to fifteen minutes at a time, can actually alter your perception. The positive mental energy will start to work in your favor, as it did for my client, who became progressively more confident during his sales pitches.

Imagine the bad along with the good. I know I've hammered home the importance of keeping a positive mind-set, and I do believe that the balance of your visualization should be about imagining how to perform a task optimally. But you should also prepare for worst-case scenarios. What if your computer breaks down right before the meeting? Or if the must-land client doesn't like your presentation? How will you react in those situations? Imagining yourself in effective problem-solving mode is another important component of the visualization process.

Turn your life into a film. Pretend your life is a movie and you're the director. You get to call the scenes and write the dialogue. There you are at the breakfast table, enjoying a healthy breakfast and giving the kids words of encouragement as they race off to school. Cut to the morning meeting, where you're delivering a confident summary of the work plan for the week. Now it's evening, and you're picking up a bottle of your spouse's favorite wine to make them feel special. Engage all of your senses as you imagine these scenes and really go there with your mind.

Role-play. This is another technique that I often use with clients. It requires a partner, someone you're comfortable letting go with—but if you can find that person, it takes the visualization process to a whole new level. Think of it as a sparring match. Your partner is there to ask tough questions and push you to uncomfortable places (and you're to do the same when the roles are reversed). If you're role-playing for a job interview, your partner should challenge your credentials and really make you prove yourself. If it's a new-client meeting, they should be extra skeptical of the idea you're pitching. The exercise is meant to push your limits so that you'll be prepared for any eventuality when the real situation comes around.

Jillian's Story

I like the whole life-as-a-movie exercise. It was kind of fun to imagine myself in these disastrous situations at the office. I mean, I already do prepare for worst-case scenarios. That's part of my obsessive preparation. But I never imagine it's me who's the cause of the problem. I liked picturing myself being the one screwing up the numbers in a tight negotiation. It would never happen, of course (ha-ha), but it was fun to imagine. And in all seriousness, I did see a different side of myself.

Adam's Story

As I've been thinking more about my sports day, I realize that I used to do a lot of visualization—without knowing what it was. In baseball, especially, I can remember standing in the on-deck circle and in between pitches, I'd close my eyes and imagine swinging through the ball, making clean contact, then watching the ball sail over the fence or up the middle. I'm sure one of my coaches taught us the technique. But it all came back to me. And I realize I still do it in certain situations, like before giving a presentation at work. So it's good to know I have some experience with visualization. The trick now is being able to apply it to other, more challenging situations.

DAVE'S STORY

This is another tough one for me, because the truth is, if I ever visualize anything, it's usually the opposite of success. I'll visualize a presentation going poorly, people looking at me like I'm crazy when I ask them for things, public speaking engagements ending in disaster. But I don't usually visualize success. So this will be a new muscle that I'm working, for sure. But it makes sense, because none of those bad things that I imagined ever actually happened. That doesn't mean the opposite played out, but the worst-case scenario that I had in mind was definitely a figment of my imagination. So I'm excited to see what this new form of mental preparation brings.

STEP SEVEN: DEVISE A PROGRAM

The final step of Hell Week preparation is really an amalgamation of the first six. You've prepared mentally and thought about what it means to embrace adversity. You've considered your fitness and dietary habits. You've solicited feedback from key people in your life and incorporated what they said into the formulation of specific goals. You've visualized what success will look like. Now it's time to pull it all together and devise a plan for the seven days that are Hell Week.

When I work one-on-one with clients, they are sometimes taken aback when they learn that it's up to them to create their plan—especially those who lead unstructured lives by nature. "You mean you're not going to tell me what to do?" they ask. I understand their concern, and if you're suddenly feeling a little unmoored, I understand yours.

Relax. Devising a plan for Hell Week doesn't mean scheduling every second of every day. Life is way too unpredictable for that level of detail. But as you prepare for the best, most productive week you've had in years, or ever, you can't just leave it all to chance. The exact nature of your schedule will depend on the goals you're looking to achieve. For example, if you're seeking a career change, I want you to schedule meetings or calls this week with at least three people from places where you'd like to work. If your primary goal is to improve your marriage and family life, you will need to plan a date night with your spouse and special activities with your children. If you want to start writing the novel that's been bouncing around in your head for years, this is the week you will finally sign up for that writing course.

In addition to tending to major issues in your life, your Hell Week plan should anticipate any distractions that might crop up over the course of the next week. These energy leakages, as I call them, threaten to sap your momentum and prevent you from pulling off the perfect week. They might be minor administrative matters, like paying the bills or scheduling a doctor's appointment. In the past, you'd avoid them and they would linger in the back of your mind, taking mental energy away from the thinking and ideas that matter most. This week, you will plan a specific time to deal with them, so that they don't leak energy away from your larger goal.

The best Olympic athletes I've worked with, like the wrestler Stig-André Berge or the taekwondo practitioner Nina Solheim, have the minutiae down to a science. Twenty-four-hour athletes in the truest sense of the word, they spent every day and night looking for ways to optimize their performance. They got better at planning their days and weeks, which helped them to prioritize their activities. They slept and rested optimally to restore their energy. They listened to their bodies and adjusted their training accordingly. They learned to enjoy nonsport activities because they recognized the role they played in recharging their batteries. They paid attention to feedback from their training managers and support teams. Most athletes know what they ought to do. Stig-André and Nina actually did it.

People often think of mental training solely in terms of the performance, but really it's about the preparation. And proper preparation is about all of the everyday habits and routines that many people forget to think about but that are decisive pieces in the grand scheme of things. The outcome of the game is decided in advance by everyday life, where seemingly trivial details separate the winners from the also-rans. Here's how to come up with a fail-proof plan for Hell Week.

THE ACTION PLAN

Put your life into perspective. You will have begun this process already, especially during the goal-defining phase of your Hell Week preparations. But as you devise your actual plan for the week, I want you to focus hard on the finality of life. This may strike you as somewhat morbid, but I call this process the philosophizing of death. Recognizing that one day you will lie in your grave can affect your gratitude for being alive now. And it's a pretty good motivator, too.

Tackle the big stuff first. As you devise your daily agenda for Hell Week, front-load your day with the bigger, more demanding tasks or assignments. A lot of people make the mistake of whittling away the early morning hours with busywork, like checking email. All this week, I want you to start out with something big and challenging. So much the better if it's something you've been putting off for a while. You'll find that crossing major items off your to-do list early in the day will give you a big push of momentum.

Stay flexible. Contingency plans are the stuff of highly success-ful planners. Apart from the 5:00 a.m. wake-up call, the rest of your Hell Week schedule will be subject to the vagaries of life, from sick children to jackknifed tractor trailers on the freeway that leave traffic snarled for miles. Life happens, it's true, so you need to be ready with plan B. Remain proactive, not re-active, so that even if you have to shift course during the week, you can stay focused on the goals at hand. A combination of flexibility and persistence will see you through the week.

Identify energy sources. I talked above about energy leakages—those aspects of your life that slow you down or distract you from the task at hand. As you chart your Hell Week, I want you to become aware of environments and activities that have the opposite effect. Exercise is perhaps the greatest energizer, and it's automatically programmed into your week's routine. What else inspires and motivates you? You should schedule at least two hours of these activities into your Hell Week.

Be ready to say no. A study from the University of California in San Francisco found that people who have a hard time saying no tend to experience higher levels of stress, burnout, and even depression. Makes sense, right? If you accept every assignment that comes your way, it's only a matter of time before the over-load sets in. As you set your priorities for the week, get ready to decline any offers or requests that will get in the way. Practice saying no with confidence. Mentally tough people steer clear of phrases like "I don't think I can" or "I'm sorry to disappoint," and instead opt for more forceful language like "I can't do it" or "You'll have to find someone else." Remember, it's healthy to say no.

Find time for fun. Hell Week is going to be hard work, but you shouldn't dread it. Give yourself rewards each day and plan something extraspecial for the end of the week, whether it's cracking open that prized bottle of wine or going out for a meal at your favorite restaurant. I can still remember the single square of milk chocolate that I received from the commanding officer during my military Hell Week. I still think about it every time I eat chocolate. Challenging situations and difficult times produce a heightened sense of gratitude. You will learn a great deal from the contrasts within Hell Week.

Employ daily affirmations. If you're the humble kind, this one might make you squeamish. But daily affirmations are a device used by many successful and mentally resilient individuals. During Hell Week, I want you to spend a few minutes each day reminding yourself why you're a damned good person. Focusing on your strong suits is one of the best ways to develop a stronger sense of self.

DAVE'S STORY

Hell Week is all about a career change for me, so I've got my appointments set up—the guy I grew up with who works at a big new-media company; an old colleague from my last job, just to see what other opportunities might be there; and my first meeting with a headhunter, to find out what that's all about. It should be interesting.

JILLIAN'S STORY

I'll consider Hell Week a major victory if I say no to just one unreasonable demand at the office and have one extra laugh with friends. Okay, maybe I need to set the bar a little higher. But I'll start the program with those two items and then go from there.

ADAM'S STORY

Obviously I'm not going to drop fifty pounds in a week. But I want to take this opportunity to really chart a new path to wellness, once and for all. I'm hyperfocused on doing the two workout sessions each day. I've set up a few sessions throughout the week with friends to help keep me on track, but I know the rest will have to come from within. I'm not sure how that's going to go. The healthy diet is the other big component of my program. I've cleared the house of junk food and soda and stocked up on fresh fruits and vegetables and nuts and stuff, following Erik's advice. Just getting that temptation out of the way has been empowering. Staying out of bars and restaurants all week will serve a similar purpose, though I might reward myself with a meal out on Sunday, assuming I do hit all the marks throughout Hell Week.

PART TWO

HERE COMES HELL WEEK

ACT AS IF WHAT YOU DO MAKES A DIFFERENCE. IT DOES. —WILLIAM JAMES

Welcome to Hell Week. For the next seven days, every act you commit will most definitely make a difference, and I believe it will be an immensely positive one. There are many facets of mental training, but they all come back to this one simple principle: by raising your level of consciousness so that your every action becomes deliberate, a matter of choice and free will, you will lead a better, more productive life. It's really no more complicated than that.

I have tremendous faith in the human spirit, and I believe we can squeeze more out of life than we ever thought possible. Think for a moment about the progress we've made as a civilization—sending spaceships to the moon and Mars, developing a computer that fits in the palm of your hand, curing all manners of once life-annihilating disease. Each of the milestones started with one simple idea, often in the mind of one man or woman, though of course they would have plenty of help along the way: Steve Jobs tinkering in his garage, Louis Pasteur experimenting in the laboratory, President Kennedy vowing to "land a man on the moon and return him safely to the Earth" by the end of the 1960s.

Each of us is capable of living more intensely, more success-fully, and enjoying more of life's fantastic moments. The choice is ours. We can continue to develop and to learn. We can form dreams and chase them down. First, however, we must bring these goals to the forefront of our minds. This is the meaning of Hell Week.

On Monday, we'll establish a new level of consciousness with regard to habits. On Tuesday, we'll turn to focus, concen-tration, and moods, or "modes," as I like to call them. Wednes-day will force you to think deliberately about your use of time. Come Thursday, we'll face your fears head-on. On Friday, we'll learn how to rest with purpose. Saturday we'll turn inward. And Sunday will be a day of focused perspective.

This is the program I've developed through years of mental training, working with hundreds of clients of all ages and walks of life. I believe it uses the major skills and faculties needed to live an optimal life. The program is designed to be self-reinforcing. The work on habits that you do on Monday will lead to positive modes, which in turn will allow you to manage your time better, and so on. Of course, Hell Week is just the beginning. The skills you learn over the next seven days will need to be refined in the weeks, months, and years to come.

Beyond the seven daily themes, there are a series of rules that you must live every day. Think of them as your basic train-ing. In the military, most soldiers eventually specialize in one particular area—paratrooping, in my case. But all soldiers must also learn a basic set of skills, such as marksmanship and teamwork. The same is true for civilian Hell Week. With that, here are the rules that you will adhere to all day, every day.

THE SEVEN RULES OF HELL WEEK

To win at Hell Week, you need to bring your A-plus-plus game. There's no margin for error here, no "I need to sleep in this morning" or "I really want to meet friends for a drink after work today." In the military version of Hell Week, I saw guys get reprimanded all the time for the smallest infractions. Maybe they'd fall asleep during their watch, which can obviously have huge consequences on the field of battle. Or they'd leave behind something minor, like a sock or water bottle. A slipup that small could be enough to send them packing.

My Hell Week isn't quite so severe. But I demand a lot. Do you like to check your email on your phone before you go to bed each night? Not this week you don't. Fond of hitting the snooze button a few times before you finally roll out of bed? Not on my watch. Each day of Hell Week has a specific theme, an area of your life on which I need you to be hyperfocused. But there are certain rules that apply across the entirety of Hell Week, from 5:00 a.m. Monday morning until 10:00 p.m. Sunday night, when I expect you to collapse in a heap of fatigue and satisfaction. With that, here are your seven rules of Hell Week.

RULE NUMBER ONE: EARLY TO BED (10:00 P.M.), EARLY TO RISE (5:00 A.M.)

Yeah, I know, you've been hearing that since you were five years old. So why hasn't it stuck? At least you're not alone. Somewhere between fifty million and seventy million Americans don't get enough sleep to the point where it significantly affects their health, alertness, and safety. Not impressed by that fact? Try this one on for size: a recent study found that getting an extra hour of sleep per week (not per day, mind you, per week) can increase wages by more than 4 percent. Not a bad little raise for simply giving your mind and body the essential rest they need.

There is one major exception to this rule during Hell Week that I have to point out here. It happens on Thursday, when I'll ask you to skip sleep altogether and spend all night engaged in productive work. I'll cover this in more detail later in the book. For now, consider yourself forewarned.

RULE NUMBER TWO: LOOK YOUR ABSOLUTE BEST AT ALL TIMES

You've probably heard the old adage "Dress for the job you want, not the one you have." During Hell Week, I want you to extend that to your entire life. That doesn't mean you have to rush out and buy a new wardrobe for Hell Week, but I do want you to go up a notch with your clothes and appearance, so that you're looking your absolute best when you walk out of your home each morning—hair neatly brushed, shirt or blouse ironed, fingernails clipped or neatly manicured.

I even want you to take special care of your appearance when you're knocking around the house. Impress your spouse or your kids, or even just the family pet. Hell Week is about establishing new patterns of behavior. Sometimes a "fake it till you make it" philosophy applies, and upping your appearance is one of those times.

RULE NUMBER THREE: EXERCISE TO THE EXTREME

I can't remember the last time I met a highly successful person who didn't work out regularly. There's an inextricable link between physical fitness and mental health, which in turn allows for peak performance and productivity. During Hell Week, I want you to take this principle to the extreme by exercising every day for a minimum of one hour. You can choose to do two thirty-minute sessions—a good option for very busy people or for those who aren't yet in top physical shape. At least two of the exercise sessions during the week must be extremely vigorous, relative to your current level of fitness. If you usually run 5Ks in forty minutes, I want you to run a 10K in under an hour. If you've only ever done the beginner's spin class, go for the intermediate or advanced. Hell Week is all about pushing your limits (as much as your health and doctor permit), and physical activity is one of the best opportunities to do so.

RULE NUMBER FOUR: STICK TO A HEALTHY DIET

Along with sleep and exercise, a healthy diet forms the three-legged stool that's essential for a sound mind and body. I want you to forget the traditional three-squares-per-day model and instead eat more frequently throughout the day—say, five smaller meals, two of which should be snacks. I don't like to get too prescriptive with the actual menu planning, since people often have dietary restrictions or strong preferences for certain types of foods. But generally speaking, I have clients stock up on easy-to-prepare items, including eggs, fruits and vegetables, nuts, granola, yogurt, and grains. There is no shortage of advice out there on creating a healthful diet. The important thing is that you do it.

Of course, all kinds of junk food—including potato chips, soft drinks, and chocolate—are strictly forbidden during Hell

Week. I also insist that you don't use alcohol. These are big sacrifices for people—and that's exactly the point.

RULE NUMBER FIVE: TAKE CHARGE OF YOUR DIGITAL LIFE

Smartphones and tablet computers were supposed to simplify life, but for many of us, they've resulted in digital overload. It's just not possible to keep up with so many information streams—from email to your Twitter feed to your friends on Facebook—and still be productive in the areas that matter, namely work and personal relationships with family and friends. Hell Week will force you to break the harmful digital habits that have likely crept into your life in recent years.

This will require several measures. First, you will not use social media in any personal form during work hours. I realize that many people's jobs now require them to be on Twitter and Facebook. If that includes you, I need you to be disciplined and not take a detour into your old college friend's Instagram page.

Last but not least, you will not watch television during Hell Week. Don't worry, your favorite show will be there a week from now (though I hope any tendency to binge watch will be gone, or at least greatly reduced).

RULE NUMBER SIX: GET HYPERFOCUSED

If you work in an office, you have a natural separation between work and home life. But technology has done a lot to blur the line. Per rule number five, think about how many times you check your Facebook page at the office, or your work email at home. In fact, this rule has a lot to do with managing digital distractions, but it goes even further. During Hell Week, I need you to make a conscious effort to make work only about work. Text messages, phone calls, and emails to friends during office hours (whatever those may be for you) are forbidden. Conversely, when you walk through the door at the end of the day, you need to be 100 percent focused on your home life. If you have a family, give them your undivided attention. If an evening workout is part of the routine, pour yourself into that. Your goal is to make it to about 9:00 p.m., when it's time to get into bed with something to read, preparing your mind and body for a solid night's sleep.

RULE NUMBER SEVEN: STEP UP YOUR GAME

This is the most amorphous of the seven rules, but it's also the most important, which is why I like to end with it. Hell Week is a test of your will and mental fortitude. You've got to be in it all the way. I've had clients give me less, and in every case the return was less than it could have been. Those Hell Weekers who do go all out, without exception, come away from the experience with a renewed focus and direction. So what exactly does staying the course involve? I'll return to the theme throughout this book, but it boils down to the following principles:

Hard work. Whether you're completing an important assignment at work or simply folding the laundry, I need you to tackle every task with purpose and resolve.

Dedication. As a follow-up to hard work, I also need you to see every task through. Modern life makes it very easy to slip into a start-and-stop rhythm, where you end up getting very little done. Even if it means taking on fewer projects, the ones you do commit to this week must be completed.

Proactivity. Don't wait for things to happen to you. Be the agent of change. Maybe there's an important conversation that you and your spouse or partner have been putting off. Or you and your colleagues have been batting around a new idea at work. Take charge of the situation and see that the idea finally comes to fruition and reaches the right people. This is the week to get it done!

Positivity. You will stay pleasant, positive, and solution-oriented at all times. When we think of a hardworking, take-charge person, he or she often looks like a real ballbuster. It doesn't have to be like that. You can be hyperproductive and still treat people with decency and respect.

Focus. I need you to be aware and conscientious of everything you do this week. Pay particular attention to the role you're playing in different situations. There are times to talk and there are times to listen. There are times to lead and there are times to follow. Be conscious of which role is required of you in any current moment, and embrace it.

It's a lot to take in, I know. Following every rule will not be easy, and that's precisely the point. Remember the words that opened this book: you can take a lot more than you think. But you need to push yourself to that limit. In a sense, we have it easier in the military, in that we have our commanding officers barking orders and forcing us to carry on. For you, that motivation must come from within. But I know you can do it. And while I won't be there in the flesh, my words are here to guide and inspire you. Okay, it's go time.

MONDAY: HARNESSING THE FORCE OF HABIT

Hell Week begins with an intense meditation on habits because, as Aristotle taught, "We are what we repeatedly do." Within minutes of meeting a person, I can identify their defining habits, good and bad. If it's a scheduled appointment, the person who arrives on time is likely in the habit of being punctual, while the one who turns up late is probably tardy a lot. A firm handshake and direct eye contact are habits that help form a positive first impression, compared with a limp shake and averted gaze. Then there's physical appearance. I can tell not only if a person exercises regularly, but also whether they do so for strength, endurance, or some combination of the two. Hygiene is yet another manifestation. Carefully manicured nails and sparkling teeth are signs of someone who is in the habit of caring for his or her appearance.

We are indeed what we repeatedly do. Aristotle's teaching goes on to posit that "Excellence, then, is not an act but a habit." You don't hear that quote cited as often, but I think it contains the real wisdom within this Aristotelian idea—and it's the reason, again, that Hell Week opens with a thorough review of the habits that define your life. Habits regulate be-havior, determine priorities, dictate choices, and they do all this without your full awareness. That's the point Aristotle was making. One doesn't achieve excellence by making the decision in his or her mind to do so and then following through with it. Excellence is not a conscious act, but rather the result of habits that are cultivated over time.

Mind you, this is a very deliberate process. Habits even-tually become second nature, but they are born not by acci-dent, but out of your own free will. We are not born biting our nails, for example. This behavior pattern, like others, is learned through repetition until an unconscious habit is established. But just as habits are learned, they can be unlearned.

I think here of a professional hockey player with whom I had the honor of training. He possesses incredible talent, in-cluding almost preternatural hand-eye coordination. But it's the diligence of his training that elevated his game. I'm a pretty disciplined guy, and even I was in awe of his relentless pursuit of perfection, the countless hours he put in on the ice and in the gym.

Athletes often talk about muscle memory, whereby a spe-cific motor task (swinging a golf club, for example, or throwing a split-finger fastball) is repeated often enough that the body is able to perform it without conscious effort. The hockey player has some of the strongest muscle memory of any athlete I've ever observed. But that by itself didn't catapult him to the game's highest level. He had to bring the mental excellence of his game in line with the physical. That was a big part of the work we did together, because despite all his raw talent and ability, he could be prone to bouts of self-doubt. It's a habit shared by many top athletes.

"Where do these negative thoughts come from?" I asked during one of our early sessions.

"They just pop into my mind," he answered.

"Wrong," I said. "You let them in."

I could tell he was somewhat taken aback, as my clients often are when I make them responsible for their own challenges— especially those who have had to deal with their share of tough stuff in their lives. I understand that. And I don't mean to say to these clients (or to you) that they are the cause of their insecurity or self-doubt. They are, however, in control of these feelings. They can choose to let them in or they can choose to block them out. In the case of the hockey player, he sometimes made the choice to listen to the negative voices in his head. At times, when he fired the puck, he was letting the voices in. And some negative thinking was becoming routine. It was becoming a habit.

"What if, in the days before your next big game, you decide to only think the right thoughts?" I asked the next time we met. We talked about what this might look like. During practice, he would focus on what worked, rather than on what didn't. When thinking about the other team, he would picture the players he'd beaten and not the ones who had topped him. The morning of the game, he would force himself to think about how great it would be to come home a winner.

The hockey player agreed, though I could tell he was skeptical. After all, it wasn't like I identified some problem in his slap-shot or introduced him to a new kind of skates. The changes he agreed to were, however, just as fundamental. Sure enough, as his right thinking became more routine, and eventually habitual, his game steadily improved.

"I have much more security now," he later told me. "I dare to do things I would not have done before, because I would have felt uncomfortable. I'm not afraid to fail anymore."

I loved hearing that. To overcome the fear of failure is a major achievement for anyone, let alone a professional athlete who must push himself nearly every day of his life. But as you just heard, the method for overcoming that fear was actually quite simple. By becoming aware of his habits, the hockey player was able to identify a negative behavior and turn it on its head. Through sheer force of habit, he was able to achieve excellence. Starting today, it's your turn to do the same.

I never could have done what I have done without the habits of punctuality, order, and diligence, without the determination to concentrate myself on one subject at a time. —CHARLES DICKENS

RISE AND SHINE

The assessment of habits begins in the first waking moment of Hell Week, with the sounding of the alarm at 5:00 a.m. on Monday. Imagine this moment now in your mind's eye. The room is draped in shadows. There's a chill in the air, especially if it's during the winter months. And apart from the beeping of the alarm clock, there's perfect stillness, as the world outside remains in its predawn slumber.

Your first impulse, like that of most people, will be to hit the snooze button and enjoy another ten minutes of sleep—or twenty or thirty, depending on how many times you hit the button. This desire to postpone getting out of bed in the morning is one of the most ingrained of all human habits. In the military, it's one of the first to be broken, often quite rudely, with an assortment of noisemakers, from sirens to banging pots, or for serious holdouts, the dreaded bucket of ice water.

You won't have to contend with such tortures, though depending on the depth of your sleeping-in habit, that could make the challenge of getting up all the more difficult. But let's try to understand what's actually happening in this moment. Your body is asleep, your pulse rate is slow, and your whole being is in standby mode. Then, *bam!* The alarm rings. As you awaken, the first thing you do is to check how you're feeling. You let your body tell you what you should think about the situation you're in. And what does your body say? It says, of course, that you should remain asleep, since you're tired. You obey your body, hit the snooze button, and sleep on.

Over the years, the action forms into an unshakable habit—or so it seems. Your first challenge of Hell Week is to break this habit. It's easier than you think, and no, it doesn't require enlisting in the military. It does, however, involve a dramatic shift in mind-set. Here's what I mean. When faced with the challenge of becoming an early riser, most people believe they simply need to force their body out of bed. In that moment when their body is telling them they should stay asleep, they try to match it with a greater amount of will. It's a valiant effort, and it might even work for a series of days or weeks. But eventually, the pendulum will swing back in the body's favor and the snooze button will resume its steady workout.

What went wrong? The person failed to change their way of

thinking about the situation. More than anything in the world, they still want those additional ten minutes of sleep. The only difference is that they began forcing themselves to override the desire. They beat back the habit, but the habit was still there.

What if they chose to create a new habit instead, the way the hockey player chose to think positive thoughts before playing, instead of negative ones? That's the strategy I want you to deploy. It begins with a clear, tangible break from the past, something as simple as placing your alarm clock in a different corner of the room. Or if you use the alarm on your phone, choose a different ringtone. These simple changes will be enough to signal to your mind that you are entering a new behavior pattern. But you must be very conscious of them. If you have a spouse or partner, inform him or her of your new practice. On Sunday night before you get into bed, focus on the new location of the clock or listen to the new ringtone. Really internalize the changes.

The big shift will take place at 5:00 a.m., when the alarm sounds. In those first seconds of consciousness, I want you to ask yourself this one simple question: What am I most looking forward to today? Since this first day will be the kickoff of Hell Week, your answer will perhaps be geared toward the challenge of it. But in the days and weeks to come, the answers will become more mundane—a dinner date planned with an old friend, an important meeting at work, or even just the cup of coffee that awaits you at breakfast. As this quick predawn ritual becomes routine, the habit will form and the question will start to pop into your head automatically the moment your alarm rings. You'll be like Pavlov's dog, only instead of salivating over the prospect of a meal, it will be the events of the day that you look forward to at the sound of your alarm clock. Indeed, I reckon you'll be at least 10 percent lighter in your mind because your focus will be pointed in a positive direction. Rather than fighting the urge to sleep, you will replace it with a new habit centered on positive mental training.

As you can tell, I'm a strong proponent of getting an early jump on the day. I really believe it builds character. But in the context of Hell Week, it's also such a perfect illustration of the power of mental training. Very few people enjoy getting up at 5:00 a.m. It is an uncomfortable state, even an unnatural one. But if you are able to establish this new habit using the simple technique I just described, you'll have a huge advantage when it comes to addressing and improving the other habits in your life.

CHARTING YOUR HABITS

Okay, you're out of bed. Hell Week is officially under way. You will adhere to the seven overarching rules for the week, from eating healthful meals to exercising regularly to being in bed by 10:00 p.m. Your unique task for Monday, in keeping with the theme for the day, will be to chart your habits—the good and the bad—so that you can bring them out of the murky depths of the subconscious and into the light of day.

Some habits will be mundane, such as the way you brush your teeth or when you check your Twitter feed on your phone. Others will be more mental, like what you say to yourself before going into a meeting or how you react to unforeseen obstacles. To begin, I simply want you to make a note of each habit as it enters your consciousness. Don't worry about assigning valuations at this stage. Just get as many habits down on paper or the computer screen as you can.

Here's a list of questions that I've compiled over the years, based on interactions with clients over their positive and negative habits.

Do you like to sing in the shower?

Do you floss your teeth after brushing?

Do you pluck your eyebrows and check the hair in your nostrils and ears?

Do you apply makeup the same way each day?

Do you put out your outfits the night before?

Do you iron your clothes?

Do you skip breakfast?

Do you walk with upright posture or are you prone to stooped shoulders?

Do you leave your dirty dishes in the sink?

Do you make your bed each morning?

Do you greet colleagues on your way into work?

Do you plan your day, or do you take things as they come?

Do you take action when you feel yourself starting to get fed up or tired?

Do you have a limp handshake?

Do you often forget the name of the person you're greeting?

Do your eyes wander when you meet new people?

Do you use social media for personal reasons during the working day?

Do you listen sufficiently in conversations and meetings?

Do you see the people around you?

Do you get to work on assignments immediately, or do you
   postpone them?

Do you eat snacks to keep your energy levels high?

Do you ask for help when you need it?

Do you work hard and effectively?

Do you ignore emails or forget to respond?

Do you listen to podcasts or audiobooks in the car?

Do you listen closely to your children?

Asking yourself these questions should help bring many of your habits from the subconscious realm up to the surface. I also want you to solicit feedback from people in your life, using the skills you developed during the feedback phase of your Hell Week preparation. Ask your spouse, close friend, and work colleagues what habits they observe in you. Be sure to get perspectives from all spheres of your life. And remember, you're not allowed to argue any of the points you hear. If a colleague tells you that you often seem checked out in meetings or that you have a habit of talking over people, I want you to nod and smile, chart the response without objection, and move on to your next interview. The same goes if your kids say your hair is a mess on weekends and you're constantly checking email on your phone, instead of listening when they talk or ask you for things. If your spouse tells you you're a noisy eater, accept the feedback without protest and note it in your chart. Hopefully, there will be some positive responses in there as well!

Chances are you won't be able to get to everyone in a single day. Likewise, it may be later in the week or month or even year that other habits appear to you. That's perfectly fine. As

I've said, Hell Week is merely the beginning of the journey. By the end of Monday, however, you should have a pretty good list of habits.

The next step in the process is to evaluate them. Find a quiet hour, perhaps after work but before you reach home, where you can review the habits in full and put them in two piles: the good and the bad. Some will be obvious. Texting while driving? Definitely a bad habit. Responding promptly to emails? Clearly a good one. Other habits may require a little more analysis. For example, many of my clients are women who struggle with what's known in Norway as the "clever girl syndrome." It's basically an extreme form of perfectionism in which they hold themselves up to the highest standard in all spheres of their life, including work, family, and friends. On the surface, striving for excellence may not seem like such a bad thing. But these women (and I see plenty of clever boys, too) end up losing the ability to distinguish between what actually has to be perfect and what simply needs to be good enough. Eventually, they end up running themselves into the ground. Clever girl syndrome belongs in the negative habit pile, even though at first glance it might look like a positive.

Once you've sorted through all your habits, dividing them into two piles, you can begin the process of reinforcing the positive habits and replacing the negative ones. Obviously this doesn't happen overnight. But you will officially begin the process on the Monday of Hell Week. Keep in mind that habits are not instinctive. They are acquired through repetition. Now that you've identified the negative habits in your life, you're in a position to unlearn them.

The work of the mental trainer often dwells on the

importance of small, everyday details and how making even slight improvements can lead to enormous positive change. Top athletes have to think like this all the time, because they are already so good at what they do. It's only in the details that they still have room for improvement. Habits and details are really two sides of the same coin. Many habits are difficult to change, but if you succeed, your life will be measurably better. Hell Week hastens this process. By turning extra focus onto your habits, and by working in a targeted way on altering them, I believe you will achieve real progress in one week. You will establish momentum in the process, and you'll realize that change doesn't cost as much as you thought or feared.

The second half of a man's life is made up of nothing but the habits he has acquired during the first half. —FYODOR DOSTOYEVSKY

DOING THE WORK

I talked a lot about emotions in the planning section of this book, specifically about the positive role emotions play in determining our actions. The feel-good factor—or *godfølelse,* as we call it in Norway—looms large in the formation of positive habits. A key goal of Hell Week is to create a support system that will enable you to develop habits of excellence. Remember Aristotle: excellence is not an act, but a habit.

So how will you actually go about changing your habits? It starts by listening to your feelings. That can be a tough sell for some people, especially hypermasculine types who don't put a lot of stock in emotions. But trust me when I say that feelings are essential to mental training and they're one of the best tools in your arsenal for changing habits. That's because habits of excellence have to do with those aspects of your inner self that you want to draw out for all the world to see: having a positive attitude and belief in your own abilities; taking care of yourself; supporting your friends and building their self-esteem and self-confidence; not taking yourself too seriously; daring to trust your own instincts; working toward your goals and your dreams; developing empathy.

Emotion is the strongest impetus for human change. Often it's rooted in a painful experience. Imagine you're passed over for a promotion at work. The feeling can be so painful and degrading that you embark on a better regimen, implementing habits that will lead to other career opportunities. Or if you're suddenly breathless walking up the stairs at the office and a colleague makes a sarcastic comment, it might hurt your feelings enough to encourage you to start exercising. These types of experiences, and the painful feelings they elicit, can be incredibly effective motivators. As you take stock of your life during Hell Week, and the habits that inform it, I want you to pay close attention to the feelings that surround them. Ask yourself: Am I living the life I always wanted? Where will I be in one year, five years, and ten years? If you don't like the answers, take the opportunity of Hell Week to shake loose from any bad habits that are getting in the way of your goals.

The second technique for changing habits is less about emotion and more about sheer determination. If you can't summon up any of the deep feelings needed for immediate change, you'll have to take the long route, making small adjustments that ultimately lead to transformation. I call this the one-minute plan.

Let's say that you want to exercise more but can't find the

motivation—you haven't had the snide comment from a co-worker as you struggle up the stairs or a grave health report from your doctor. One minute can be enough to get you on the path. Think about it: for just one minute out of the 1,440 minutes in a twenty-four-hour period, you'll devote yourself to exercise. How many push-ups can you manage in that time? How many stairs can you climb? One minute is the start. The next day go for a second minute, then a third. After a month you're up to thirty minutes. After two months you'll have reached the typical target of an hour-long workout. This same technique can be applied to all aspects of your life.

As the Monday of Hell Week comes to a close, spend a few moments reflecting on everything you accomplished, going back to the instant some seventeen hours prior when you bounced out of bed in the darkness of dawn. Hopefully that was the first of several small victories you achieved this day. Even if you only identified one bad habit that you're committed to changing, you will be on your way to a more effective and goal-oriented life geared toward the pursuit of excellence. Now get some sleep. Another challenge is just seven hours away.

Dave's Story

I managed to get out of bed by 5:00 a.m. I'm an early riser by nature (as is our three-year-old son), so it wasn't so bad. I had a tougher time with the sit-ups and push-ups that followed, but I wanted to get in the morning exercise. Then, over a cup of coffee, I sat down to write out the list of good and bad habits. It was definitely an interesting exercise. I think any success I've had in my working life is due to a few basic habits, especially meeting deadlines, being on time, working hard, and caring about my appearance. Regular exercise is another good habit I've always had, along with showing affection for my family—good-bye kisses, saying "I love you," etc.

So those are the good habits. The list of bad habits is a bit longer, but I think I can get rid of a lot of them just by being more aware. For example, I sleep with the phone and computer on the bedside table and end up checking them in the middle of the night. I'll keep them somewhere else. I hope that will help break the pre-bed TV habit, which I look forward to replacing with reading. I also check social media too much during the day, including while I'm driving(!). So I need to put the phone away. My desktops—both the digital one on the computer and the real-life one in my office—are pretty disorganized. That will be harder to fix, but I think with daily organizing it will improve, too.

Adam's Story

Whoa, that was an early wake-up call! But I got up and actually walk-jogged for two miles through pitch-dark streets. I was cursing every step of the way, but I did it. Later in the day I used Erik's list to chart out my habits. It was a pretty interesting process. Obviously, I have fairly piss-poor eating habits, but I never really examined them closely. Little habits, like taking my coffee with milk and sugar, jumped out at me. Or how there's almost always a bag of candy or chips or a sports drink in the car, which I reach for inevitably anytime I'm sitting in traffic. Basically I do a lot of mindless eating throughout the day. I feel like if I just eliminated that one bad habit, it would point me in a better direction. Then there's the bigger stuff, like how I'll think nothing of plowing through a plate of hot wings and washing it down with a few beers while watching the football game with friends. That wasn't even a good idea in college. It's definitely not smart at this age. But you know, it's just become part of the routine.

Jillian's Story

I feel like the person in the job interview here who responds to the question about weaknesses they might have by saying they're a perfectionist. But the truth is, I didn't come up with any explicit bad habits. I don't drink or smoke or overeat. I drive the speed limit. I answer important emails right away.

I'm not saying I'm perfect. I wouldn't have signed up for Hell Week if that was the case. But it doesn't look like eliminating bad habits is necessarily the answer. Or if it is, I'll have to look deeper into the behavior patterns for bad habits that are less on the surface.

TUESDAY: GETTING INTO THE MODE

Welcome to Tuesday. Monday was given to a full assessment of your existing habits. Day number two of Hell Week is all about developing a new habit, the one I call getting into "the mode." It's the mental state that will enable you to perform at your highest optimal level, whatever the task at hand. You've probably experienced the mode throughout your life, perhaps even on a consistent basis. But very few people are in full control of this powerful mental tool, to the point where they can summon it at will. That's your challenge for today: recognize the power of the mode and learn how to channel it.

If you watch a lot of professional sports, you've seen mode in action many times, as athletes get themselves mentally prepared before a competition. "Getting into the zone" is how they sometimes describe it. Optimal performance modes take many forms. I used to love watching John McEnroe and Björn Borg battle it out on the tennis court because they had such opposing styles of mode: McEnroe hot-tempered and impetuous, Borg calm and detached. McEnroe later claimed that he tried to be more Borg-like at times, restraining his temper and biting his tongue, but he just couldn't do it. The mode didn't suit his style of play.

Or think about the contrasting modes of Mike Tyson and Muhammad Ali. Early in his career, Tyson realized that he had to be the aggressor in the ring. He boxed his best when he was at his most dangerous. Ali was the opposite. He used humor, levity, and quiet concentration to get into fight mode. In both cases, the boxers recognized that the technical aspects of their game would kick in automatically as long as they could get themselves into the right state of mind.

Usain Bolt, on many days the world's fastest man, is another interesting study in mode. If you've ever watched him before a competition, he is the picture of looseness, all smiles and jokes and laughter—very Ali-like in a sense. That's clearly the mode he's created to get himself ready for the race. More often than not, it helps him run faster than every other sprinter in the field. During the 2011 World Championship in South Korea, how-ever, a very different Usain Bolt appeared before the cameras. Instead of hamming it up as usual, he had an extremely seri-ous countenance. As he approached the starting blocks, he ap-peared to scream something at himself. It was a more Tyson-like outburst. Moments later, he made a very uncharacteristic false start and was disqualified from the 100-meter final. Just like John McEnroe trying to adopt a calmer demeanor, Bolt had taken himself out of his optimal performance mode.

MAKING SENSE OF YOUR MODES

As you move through Tuesday, I want you to pay close attention to your various modes. Nobody stays in the same state the entire day. We move in and out of different modes depending on the situation. For example, many people find it easier to concentrate in the morning, while others do their best thinking at night. Likewise, our bodies behave differently at various times throughout the day. Some periods are better for rest, some for activity.

Professional athletes have to be sensitive to this point, since they typically have a combination of daytime and evening events during a season. A 2011 study by the American Academy of Sleep Medicine found that players from Major League Baseball who were "morning types" had higher batting averages in games that started before 2:00 p.m. than players who were "evening types."

Reaching further back in history, there's the example of Winston Churchill, who was known for his ability to summon different modes with great ease and alacrity. During breaks in the intense negotiation sessions with fellow leaders of the Allied forces, Churchill liked to slip into quiet rest mode while his counterparts nervously smoked cigars on the balcony. Ten minutes later when the parties reconvened, he would awaken from his nap, fully rested and alert.

What do your modes look like? That's what I want you to figure out today. Just as you charted your habits on Monday, I want you to keep a running list of your modes as you go about your day. It should end up being a shorter list, since people typically have more habits than modes. But whereas habit charting required you to be very focused on the here and now, making note of behavioral patterns as they happen, with modes I want you to be a little more reflective. Think back over the course of your life, including childhood. What are some times when you were at your best? What were your strongest performances? When did you shine? Maybe it was a music recital you gave in high school or the standout game you played for your college volleyball team. Or perhaps it was from your first job, when you impressed your boss and colleagues with a command presentation. Hopefully there are recent examples as well—the speech you delivered to an audience of peers from your field or the composure you bring to coaching your kids' soccer team.

As your list of best performances grows, think about the mode you were in for each. It won't necessarily be identical, but I think certain common denominators will emerge. You'll realize that you are usually relaxed and jocular in your finest moments. Or you'll notice that you usually get yourself fired up before big events. Whatever your optimal mode, I want you to become keenly aware of its qualities and nuances. Modes can be quite complex. I discussed Muhammad Ali earlier, whose mode was a delicate balance between easygoing levity and intense concentration. That same balance was reflected in his fighting style. "Float like a butterfly, sting like a bee," as he liked to say.

Many of the athletes I work with have similarly multifaceted modes that need to be unpacked. That's certainly true of Stig-André Berge, the Norwegian wrestler with whom I've worked for several years. Like a lot of athletes, he had a tendency to overthink upcoming competitions.

"I get all up in my head," he told me at the beginning of our work together. "I start running through every scenario in my head, both good and bad. I think to myself, 'If I beat this opponent, I'll meet him in the next match, and then what? But if I lose, I'm out, my family will be disappointed, my trainers will be disappointed.' My mind just keeps spinning through the different outcomes."

Berge had all the talent needed to be a champion wrestler. But he wasn't getting into the proper mode before meets. We worked together to identify his optimal mode. Aggression was clearly at its core. But that alone wasn't enough to block out the distracting thoughts. He needed to add self-confidence. We worked on ways to do this, mainly through positive inner dialogue. An hour or so before his meet, I had him repeat affirmative phrases like "I'm tough, I'm bad, I'm the best wrestler ever, I am strong, I am persistent." I also had him play scenes of past victories in his head, visualizing the decisive move that took his opponent down, or the moment where he broke free from an especially solid headlock. These confidence-building techniques helped control his aggression and keep it focused. But something else was needed to complete Berge's optimal performance mode. Taking a page from Ali, we added a tinge of humor to the mode by incorporating a simple wink that he shoots at his trainer right before entering the mat. The wink lets off just enough steam to keep his focus razor sharp in the crucial seconds before the referee blows his whistle.

"When I go out onto the mat, I am much more focused than I used to be," Berge told me. "Now I don't hear a thing. I shut it all out. All I hear are these three words swirling around in my mind: aggression, calmness, wink. Those three words are my mode. Because we've rehearsed them over and over again, all I need to do is say them aloud and I'm in the mode."

That's been one of my mantras—focus and simplicity. Simple can be harder than complex: You have to work hard to get your thinking clean to make it simple. But it's worth it in the end because once you get there, you can move mountains. —STEVE JOBS

DON'T FOCUS ON THE TASK AT HAND

You read that correctly. As contradictory as it sounds, to focus on the task at hand when you are in the middle of the performance situation devalues the work and training that preceded it. Practice makes perfect—not intense levels of focus and concentration. The whole point of training is that it automatizes tasks to the point where you don't have to think about them. To turn around and become hyperfocused on these tasks is as absurd as a driving instructor forcing his student to concentrate on shifting gears instead of paying attention to the traffic ahead.

Or think about a ski jumper. As he approaches the start gate at the top of the hill, he should not be thinking about the angle of his knees during the descent or the trajectory of his impending flight. To do so will take away from the mental capacity needed to get his mind into optimal mode. If he's already nervous, those feelings will only be compounded by this last-minute technical review. The same goes for the businessperson who anxiously reviews his notes in the minutes before a big speech or presentation.

Instead of obsessing over the performance, you should be using your power of thinking and mind capacity to get yourself into the proper mode.

Like Berge, you need to figure out your optimal performance mode, and then develop a technique for accessing it. Personally, I like to get primal, thumping my chest with my fist and screaming "Come on!" I'll even assume the battle position and imagine the scene that's about to play out, whether it's a difficult conversation, placing a cold call to a new client, or stepping up to the podium to deliver a speech. My actual behavior will be different in these three situations, but the mode

I need to be in is the same, as is the technique I use to reach that state.

Michael Phelps, the greatest swimmer the world has ever seen, takes a different approach. Before each meet, he plays the same Lil Wayne song, "I'm Me," on his iPod. I'll spare you the racy lyrics, but suffice it to say it's a pretty empowering little ditty. Despite its intensity, the music and the fiery lyrics coax Phelps into a super-relaxed state. In order to swim in a way that appears effortless, Phelps knows he has to stay calm. He walks slowly toward the pool, taking in the scene with an almost lazy gaze. He touches the starting block and adjusts his swim cap. Each movement is deliberate and controlled. He knows there's no point in contemplating technique at this time. He simply focuses on being relaxed and delivering the goods. With seconds to go before the start of the race, he steps forward and stretches his arms behind his back. Then, suddenly, he slaps his arms hard across his chest. He's so flexible in his shoulders that his hands slap his back. He does it two or three times, hard and forceful. *Slap, slap, slap!* The sound is a reminder of what he needs to do now: "Swim like hell." He thinks this rather than says it out loud, in order to avoid excitement at the outset of the race. In due time, he will awaken his raw energy, but right now he has to be cool. The sound reminds him that this is actually very easy: swim like hell, nothing more, nothing less. The rest comes automatically. Now it's all about waiting for the start signal. He trusts his mode and lets the training take over. As the gun fires, Phelps enters the pool, still calm and collected. Somewhere around the halfway point of the race, he unleashes his inner beast by repeating his mantra to himself: swim like hell. That's just what he does, and many times more often than not, his fingers are the first to touch the finish line.

Notice that Berge and Phelps both rely on a phrase, or mantra as it's sometimes called, to push them into the optimal mode. This is an incredibly effective technique that I want you to consider. Known in the mental training business as "self-talk," it's the stuff we say to ourselves in the period before an event that greatly affects our performance. Go back to your list of best performances from your life. Are there certain words or objects that characterize the moments? Can you distill them into a single mantra? It might be a string of adjectives that describes your optimal mood: "fearless, focused, extreme." Or it could be a directive like, "Give it your everything."

Once you've figured out your mantra, you need to get into the habit of using it to call forth your optimal performance mode. In the beginning, that might mean repeating it fifty to a hundred times. Say the words enough, and they will start to translate into the feeling you have when you're at your best. It helps if you also attach some kind of image to your self-talk. Maybe it's the stadium in which one of your best athletic performances occurred. Or the conference room where you delivered one your strongest presentations. It could even be as simple as an object—an award you received or a hard-earned diploma. The best imagery will be evocative, including sights, smells, and sounds that help transport you into optimal performance mode.

Finally, I want you to come up with a pre-performance routine of your own. It doesn't have to be as involved as the one used by Michael Phelps or as primal as my chest-thumping regimen. But you need to establish some pattern of behavior that helps get your head in the game. Music is certainly an excellent device.

Meditation is another tool I use often to help people find their mode. The technique has gotten very trendy lately with so much attention on "mindfulness," which is usually defined as a state of open attention on the present, where you can experience your thoughts and feelings without any kind of value judgment. I don't have any problem with mindfulness, though in the context of mental training, I prefer to think of meditation as a way of clearing the mind to make way for optimal mode, whatever that might be.

Let's say a client is tense. I know that I have to remove the stress if we're going to have a productive mental training session. I'll ask her to sit down, relax, and find a comfortable position. Breathe with your diaphragm, I'll say. Close your eyes. Sit heavily in the chair. Plant the soles of both feet firmly on the ground. Relax your arms and shoulders. What do you smell? I'll ask. What do you hear? She's not to answer, but simply to focus inside her head on the smells and sounds. We'll do the exercise together. I will hear the sounds out in the street, the gulls screeching down in the harbor, the sound of my client breathing. After several minutes I will invite her to open her eyes and tell her that we can get started. (We'll come back to meditation later in Hell Week.)

Try to do a similar exercise yourself. Think back to a place where you felt completely quiet and relaxed. Find that place in your thoughts. Use all your senses and be there. The process takes only three to four minutes. When you open your eyes again, your mind will be clear, and when saying your mantra or self-talk, you may be able to transition right into performance mode.

Concentrate all your thoughts upon the work at hand. The sun's rays do not burn until brought to a focus. —ALEXANDER GRAHAM BELL

LEARNING TO CHANGE MODES

I've spent a lot of time talking about your optimal mode, because it's the most important mode to mental training, and the one you'll reach for in high-pressure situations. But it's important to understand the natural rhythm of modes.

My clients from the business world often make this mistake. I once worked with an executive at a software development firm. She was in a high-powered role that required her to be in basically nonstop meetings. Some were with her direct reports, some with fellow senior leaders, and some with potential new business partners.

"How do you prepare for these different meetings?" I asked during one of our sessions. She explained that she'd review who was going to be in the meetings, the key points she wanted to cover, and questions that might come up. Those are all important preparations, though they didn't answer my question.

"But how do you get yourself prepared mentally for these different meetings?" I asked. "What is your energy level? What is your attitude going in? What expectations do you set for yourself?"

"I don't know how to answer that," she said. "I am who I am. I don't change from one meeting to the next. I like to be constant and predictable."

It was a perfectly reasonable response, one that a lot of people would probably relate to. And yet it's the wrong approach, because it fails to take into account the variability of modes. It's simply not possible to live your entire life in optimal performance mode. You need to shift gears throughout the day. Just like a car engine, you can't run in fifth gear forever.

Many people don't recognize this. They stay in high gear for too long and burn out. Or, more often, they stay in third gear all the time, and never enter into optimal performance mode. Neither approach offers any kind of path to excellence.

Proper planning is the way to effectively manage your modes. You need to know when it's time to kick into high gear and when it's better to coast. Going back to my client, the various meetings in her calendar clearly called for different modes. She didn't need to be in high gear when she was getting routine updates from her staff. Sure, she had to stay focused and attentive and respond with energy and clarity to their questions and requests. But this wasn't a challenge situation—unlike the meeting with possible new clients, where she absolutely needed to bring her best self. By identifying the different moments in her day, she was able to plan her modes accordingly.

As Tuesday draws to a close, think about the different modes you discovered. Hopefully you were successful in identifying your optimal mode, the one you'll turn to in high-pressure situations moving forward. It will take time to refine the mode and the process you use to enter into it. That's part of the journey. Michael Phelps didn't swim like hell the first time he jumped into the pool and Muhammad Ali didn't always sting like a bee. But through their mastery of mode, they found the way. And you will, too.

Jillian's Story

I realize I have one mode and one mode only, and it's pretty hardcore. It's done a lot of good for me over the years, but I can see how it's also made certain aspects of my life more difficult. I think, for example, that my relationships with some of my family members have been strained by the take-charge attitude that I bring to those interactions. I'm the oldest, so to some extent I feel like that role has been thrust upon me, but at the same time I've never thought to question it. We're actually getting together in a few weeks to go over some estate stuff with my parents. I think it's an opportunity to take a step back and try on a less aggressive mode. Because it's not like I want to be responsible for these decisions. In fact, I'd be thrilled if one of my siblings stepped up. Maybe I just need to give them the chance.

Dave's Story

I've been paying attention to the different modes I enter into and out of throughout the day. I play a lot of soccer and I realize that my best mode is when I'm on the field, which is also when I'm happy and relaxed (my competitive playing days are over, so it's pretty casual out there). I've been trying to bring some of the lightness from the soccer field into less comfortable situations at work or in my social life. I'm pretty introverted, so I'm not a natural in these settings, but channeling my inner soccer player has helped me stay looser. I'm even keeping a soccer ball in my office to serve as a visual reminder.

WEDNESDAY: MANAGING YOUR TIME

Modern life is the scourge of time management. Once upon a time, the various compartments that made up our day-to-day existence were well defined. The workday might have been longer for some than for others, but at least it came to an end, providing a clear transition between work and home. These days, that divide is becoming increasingly blurry, thanks in large part to technology and its many devices, to which we're always tethered—smartphone, tablet, computer, laptop, and so on.

If there are kids in the picture, you need to factor in their hyperscheduled lives as well, with their sports practices and music recitals and tutoring sessions and play dates and whatever else the world today deems necessary to their happiness and success. Never mind trying to fit in a play date of your own, be it with a spouse or friend you haven't seen in months, because, well, you're both so damned busy.

Of course, I'm not telling you anything you don't know. The insanity of the modern world is pretty well documented and understood, but as we move into Wednesday of Hell Week,

I do want to change the conversation. I find it to be a little bit defeatist to suggest that the so-called "time squeeze" is simply a fact of the modern world in which we live, so we'd better get used to it. "Sheer nonsense," I say.

It's entirely possible to thrive in your career and still experience regular moments of peace, calm, and the all-important feel-good factor. You can be a capable top manager and a good mother to your children. You can be a committed entrepreneur and have a vibrant social life. You can be a high-powered hedge fund manager as well as a warm, loving, and attentive father. You can even be ill or unemployed or experiencing real hardship and still feel that you're spending your days wisely and productively.

I say this with total certainty, because I have witnessed each of those scenarios firsthand during the course of my work as a mental trainer. Like most people, my clients professed to being lousy at managing their time. It manifested in different ways. Some talked about the fact that they were constantly running late or missing appointments altogether. Others faulted their forgetfulness or their inability to prioritize. And there were those who admitted to a general loss of control.

What struck me was the sense of determinism that they all seemed to share. "I've always been absentminded," they'd say. Or, "My mother is late all the time, so it clearly runs in the family." Believing that bad time management was simply something they had to live with, they'd all gone to incredible lengths to overcompensate—to pretty remarkable effect in many cases. It didn't necessarily make my job as a mental trainer easier, since it seemed to support the argument that modern life is built on chaos and you just have to learn to deal with it, as they were doing.

Let me stop there and ask if any of this sounds familiar to you. My guess is you're doing well, superbly even, in some aspects of your life. Maybe you're succeeding in your career or raising happy, productive children or maintaining peak physical condition or enjoying a rich social life. But I'll wager that you're having trouble excelling in every area of your life. There are shortcomings somewhere, and you've accepted them as inevitable—in part because this is the view of modern life that's presented in the media. You can't have it all, the pundits and columnists and talk show hosts all insist, so be happy with what you have. This is sheer nonsense. And starting today, you're going to understand why.

A man who dares to waste one hour of time has not discovered the value of life. —CHARLES DARWIN

HITTING THE PAUSE BUTTON

Lest you think mental trainers have total control over their lives, allow me to share a recent moment from the life of Erik Bertrand Larssen. I was coming off a particularly busy stretch at work, with the usual lineup of meetings with clients, members of my staff, outside design consultants, potential book publishers, magazine reporters, and so on. It was early evening and I had ended a phone call with a new client by promising to send him some suggestions and thoughts ahead of our next session in two days. With other obligations on my mind, I pulled up the calendar on my computer to allocate time for this. As I scanned my calendar, I realized that I'd forgotten to call one of my best friends to wish him a happy birthday. The first stress bubble percolated to the surface. In the next moment, I became aware (again) of just how slow our home Internet service had become. Another stress bubble. I realized I'd forgotten to call the cable company about it. Finally my calendar loaded, only to reveal that the next two days were more or less completely booked. Bubble bubble. I'd have to work in the evening, something I promised I wouldn't do that week. Just then, my wife called out my name. "Erik, could you help me get this chest of drawers up from the basement?"

All of a sudden, the stress bubbles came to a full boil. I was officially stressed out. "Yes, of course," I said to my wife, while swearing vehemently to myself. Fortunately, though I'm not immune to this type of stress overload, I've discovered the secret to bringing it under control. It simply involves hitting the pause button.

That's what I did in that moment. I took a deep breath and committed to putting in writing everything that I had to get done. The list included tasks that were front and center, from calling the broadband provider to carrying the chest of drawers. And it included tasks that were further off, like planning a boys' weekend with my sons and developing a new business strategy for my company.

When you're feeling stressed out, making a comprehensive to-do list can feel like one more task on the pile. It's important to take a longer view and understand that hitting the pause button and regaining control is an essential part of time management. Imagine you're on a long hiking expedition and you feel the beginning of a blister on the back of your heel. It's a nuisance to have to stop the hike, remove your backpack, take off your boot and sock, and administer to the irritation. But the inconvenience is nothing compared to the pain and lost time you'll suffer if a full-scale blister develops.

Over time, you'll become more attuned to your stress loads. Quite frankly, I should have never reached the state I described above, given my training over the years. We had an expression in the military: "If you're in doubt, you're no longer in doubt." It applied to extreme, life-or-death situations—for example, during paratrooper exercises. If you have jumped out of an airplane and you discover a small tear in your parachute or several lines cut off, that should be enough for you to reach for your reserve. There shouldn't be any doubt about it.

You need to bring that same level of awareness to your stress tolerance, because you never know what's going to send that first stress bubble to the surface. If there's any doubt that you can take on another assignment at work or social engagement or favor for a friend, you need to hit the pause button. Mind you, this doesn't necessarily mean you won't be able to do the tasks. But the simple act of writing stuff down is usually enough to bring your stress levels into check.

The key is in not spending time, but in investing it. —STEPHEN R. COVEY, *THE 7 HABITS OF HIGHLY EFFECTIVE PEOPLE*

THE POWER OF POSITIVE PLANNING

The pause button is an effective tool for time management, but it's more of a stopgap measure than a way of achieving total control in your life. With that, let's move into your main challenge for the day: planning. Admittedly, that's a pretty tall order for a single day's work, especially since you still have your job to go to and exercise sessions to do and all the other demands of Hell Week. You will, however, start a process today that will put you on the path toward becoming a master planner, the benefits of which can't be overstated.

It's true—I am a huge proponent of planning. The belief is grounded in my military training, which put enormous value on planning and preparation. You've perhaps heard the expression "There's the right way, the wrong way, and the military way." In my mind, at least 90 percent of that has to do with the military's penchant for obsessive planning. You don't go into battle without plotting every coordinate, inspecting every piece of equipment, and reviewing every soldier's role, from the top brass to the lowest ranks. That's the military way. I embraced it as a soldier, and I continue to preach it as a mental trainer.

If you want to achieve greater success throughout all areas of your life, you must plan for it. That's such a basic teaching, and yet it's one that confounds so many of us. There are the fatalists, who believe their lot in life is already determined, and so what's the point in planning? There are the defeatists, who have suffered too many setbacks to believe they control their destinies. And there are the dreamers, who believe in the power of planning, but don't know how to go about it.

In each case, my advice is the same. Make planning a part of your regular routine until it forms into a habit integral to your personality. You can see again why Hell Week begins with a focused and intense examination of habits. Remember the

Aristotelian teaching from Monday: we are what we repeatedly do. Plan religiously and you will become a planner. However adverse you may be to planning today, I think you'll find you actually start to enjoy it. You'll reach a point where any failure to plan will feel uncomfortable, the same way avid exercisers get out of sorts when they miss a workout.

Plans are nothing; planning is everything. —DWIGHT D. EISENHOWER

SMART PLANNING: THE LONG AND THE SHORT OF IT

Standing before the mountain that is your life can provoke feelings of vertigo in even the most orderly individuals. If you've never been one to plan, the experience can be downright terrifying. Take a deep breath: it's not as daunting as it seems. The secret, I've found, is to start with long-term goals and progressively bring them closer to the present day. To do this, I have clients divide their planning strategy into four discrete phases: annual, monthly, weekly, and daily. This is the process I want you to begin today, getting through as much of the agenda as possible. Even if you only get so far as creating your calendar and plugging in a few goals, that will be a major step forward. I'm not too prescriptive with clients about what form the calendar should take. The more digitally minded use the calendar software on their computer, others buy a Filofax or other personal organizer, and some use nothing more sophisticated than a sheet of loose-leaf paper divided into four quadrants. Whichever system you devise, the important thing is that it remains a living, dynamic calendar that you refer to and update constantly.

THE YEARLY PLAN

Here's your thirty-thousand-foot view of the year to come, including major milestones you want to achieve and events that are either already planned or are at the top of your wish list. It's important to include both personal and professional goals in the yearly plan. So many of my clients tell me that they wish they had more time for their marriage, family, and friends. This is the moment to make those relationships a priority. Plan that trip to Paris with your spouse. Set aside time to take the kids camping. Find time for the all-girls or -boys weekend. Obviously you may need to adjust the schedule, especially if you're juggling other people's schedules. But the simple act of writing down these plans will make them a reality, as opposed to the alternative, where they linger in the back of your mind, constantly feeding those feelings of guilt we all have when we neglect the important relationships in our lives.

As for professional plans, remember the lessons from the goal-setting phase of your Hell Week preparation. They should be as specific as possible, realistic, and attainable within the twelve-month time frame. But I always want you to dare to dream. The yearly plan is a good place to test out some of your bigger ambitions. If you've been thinking about starting your own business, go ahead and put that down. If you want to make partner at your firm, include that in your goals for the year. I want you to come back to your yearly plan at least once a month, so you can always make adjustments as needed without losing sight of the ultimate goal.

THE MONTHLY PLAN

Now it's time to narrow your focus a bit, though we're not in lockdown mode yet. Too many people become prisoners of their own calendars, feeling that once something is entered there it becomes sacrosanct. One month out, you're still permitted some flexibility, even as you start to rein in your plans and objectives. As with the yearly plan, your monthly outlook should pay close attention to the important things in life. If you realize you haven't had a lot of quality time with your family, you can redress that in the weeks ahead. Or if your fitness has fallen off, you can insert extra sessions with the personal trainer or at the gym. If you're in a relationship, it's a good idea to share your monthly calendar with your partner.

One last thing: it's critical to include time for planning on the monthly planner. I repeat, it's critical to include time for planning on the monthly planner. I have clients set aside two hours in the second to last week of each month for planning. It helps to designate a special place for this—your favorite café, for example, or a quiet corner of the local library. These two hours each month are a time of reflective thinking and an opportunity to take stock of your life and put things into perspective. It should be a routine that you really look forward to.

THE WEEKLY PLAN

Let me open here with a quick story about a former client who worked as the managing director at a major pharmaceutical company. During one of our early meetings, he shared his big-picture goals about where he wanted to take the business. During the session, I asked to look at his weekly planner.

Somewhat reluctantly, he opened it up and revealed a week of wall-to-wall meetings, none of which had anything to do with his overall strategic vision.

"How do you expect to reach your goals?" I asked him. "When are you going to create the better culture you talk about and emerge as a distinctive leader when your day is consumed by meaningless meetings?" He recognized the futility of his schedule and agreed to scale back his weekly calendar, even if it meant saying no to more than a few meeting requests.

It won't be possible during Hell Week, but moving forward, you should set aside fifteen minutes on Sunday night or Monday morning to fill it out. Think about your values and goals and ensure that your week is arranged purposefully around them. If you want to exercise four times that week, put it in the planner. If you need to have an important conversation with your boss, colleague, or friend, include it. Need to catch up on time with your kids? Mark it down.

Be mindful of the lessons covered on Tuesday of Hell Week having to do with mode. I had another client who had a lot of guilt over his poor parenting. I asked him how often he saw his children and he replied that he was with them most afternoons.

"With all due respect, that's more than most people," I said. As we talked more, it became clear to me that though he was physically with his children, he was seldom really and truly present. He hadn't clarified in his head or on his calendar when he was going to be the best possible father to his kids.

The following week, he talked about an afternoon that he planned with his kids, taking them to the movies and then out to dinner. The single experience was more meaningful to him and his children than the month's worth of mindless interactions that preceded it. All he had to do was add it to the weekly agenda.

THE DAILY PLAN

In my experience, most people can handle the yearly, monthly, and even weekly plans. Maintaining a daily plan is the biggest challenge. Remember the power of habit. If you can just force daily planning into your routine, habit will take over soon enough.

You might choose to fill out your daily plan the night prior. You'll probably find you sleep better and even process some of tomorrow's challenges in your subconscious. I actually like to tackle mine first thing in the morning. I get to the office, flip on the coffee machine, and pull up my calendar.

With the daily plan, there's no more room for flexibility. In this sense, it functions more like a to-do list. These are the events and activities and tasks that you will complete before you go to bed. Once you get everything down on the to-do list, rank them from most to least important. This is critical, because you always want to start your day with the most important tasks. Your confidence will build and the sense of accomplishment will propel you through the day.

It's important to keep your daily to-do list to a realistic length. You don't want to set yourself up for failure by cramming it with items you'll never get to. If it's becoming unwieldy, look for items that can be shifted to the weekly planner. Also, look for things that can be handed off to someone else. Indeed, delegation is one of the secrets to effective time management. The ability to say no is another. I've touched on this a few times already, but it bears repeating. The most effective and efficient leaders know when they're taking on more than they can manage.

Finally, time management requires you to complete one task at a time. I opened this chapter by describing modern life as the scourge of time management. Multitasking is one of modern life's greatest fallacies. It's simply not possible to hold two thoughts in your mind at the same time, at least not with any degree of focus or concentration. The soldier who tries this in the heat of battle risks his or her life. The stakes aren't that high in civilian life, but as long as you're juggling tasks, you'll never manage your time effectively. And that will prevent you from reaching your full potential.

ADAM'S STORY

I keep thinking about the fact that I never had to think about exercise growing up because it was built into my schedule through team sports. Every day after school I was on the field or in the gym with the rest of my teammates. I never had to think about it. As an adult, I've never been able to get on that kind of schedule. What Hell Week is showing me is that I need to find some kind of structure. A few guys at work are part of a running club. They go out a couple times a week during lunch. That always seemed crazy to me, and I'm not sure I can handle it right now. But it's the sort of thing I really need to explore. I don't have enough discipline to maintain a fitness regimen over any length of time. So I'm going to seriously look for outside sources of motivation and inspiration.

JILLIAN'S STORY

I keep a pretty tight handle on my work schedule, but I can't think of the last time I planned any kind of fun. Not that I never, ever have any fun. It's just that I'm not the one who makes it happen. I've always wanted to visit Buenos Aires, so I went ahead and booked a weeklong trip there for the fall. It felt totally spontaneous even though it's not going to happen for like six months.

DAVE'S STORY

I've always thought of time management as being one of my strong suits. I'm always very punctual and I never blow a deadline. But I realized during Hell Week that I have a tendency to put things off, which creates a lot of feelings of guilt and dread. For example, my wife and I have been talking about taking a trip, just the two of us, literally for years. But we have two young kids, so it's never been a priority, which I feel bad about. As part of the yearly planner, I selected a weekend a few months out to finally make it happen. It's not going to be anything major, but just the fact that I've taken that step lifted the guilt.

As for work, I realize that I'm not very good about keeping a daily to-do list, and I often put off doing harder tasks until later in the day. As a result, I'm walking around with that feeling of dread for most of the day. So I've started making the to-do list and tackling the toughest item first. It's helped a lot with the motivation.

THURSDAY: GETTING OUT OF THE COMFORT ZONE

As Hell Week reaches its halfway point, your life should already look different from when you went to bed on Sunday. You've studied your habits, bringing them in line with your goals. You've started to master your modes, calling up the right mind-set to the day's myriad situations. You're managing your time better than ever. There's been a lot of deep thinking, but also a lot of administrative work, whipping your life into shape. Today will be different. On the Thursday of Hell Week, you will take a harder look at yourself than you've ever done before. It won't be comfortable or easy, but the potential payoff is perhaps bigger than any other day of Hell Week.

LEARNING TO SPEAK YOUR FEARS

Take a moment to think of what you fear. Do your fears feel real to you? They probably do, and there is a good reason for that: you haven't done anything about them. At the stage where you are merely thinking about your fears and not actively doing something about them, your fears have the upper hand. They own you. Starting today, you are going to do something about it, something very simple. First, I want you to list your fears out loud. This sounds silly, I know, but trust me when I say it isn't. In fact, when you think something is silly, most of the time you are actually feeling afraid of embarrassment. Tackle that fear now and speak your fears out loud.

A spoken fear tends to have a ridiculous sound to it. As long as your fear remains unspoken, it is as though you are standing in a boxing ring waiting for a mystery opponent. You know his name, but you do not know how big he will be when he finally steps through the ropes. As long as your opponent is unknown, he is an unmanageable risk. That unnerves you, and understandably so.

When you do not speak your risk out loud, you are effectively waiting in the ring. You pace the floor. You sweat. You get mentally tired. Speaking your fear forces it into the ring. And in my experience, a materialized fear is usually a pushover. Something unexpected happens when you say your fear out loud. It leaves its amorphous state in your mind and becomes something small and insignificant. When you force your fear to enter the ring by saying its name, you will find yourself saying, "I can take this guy!"

When I ask my clients what they fear, very few actually come up with a good answer. When they speak their fears out loud, they realize they don't really know why they fear them. Often, they start to see that there is actually nothing to fear. Fear is never real. It is always something we create. Like the monster under your bed that haunted your childhood, if you bend down and look under the bed, you will find no monster. If you never dare to look, you will go on being afraid.

Fear is a natural human emotion. We fear outcomes. We fear life. We fear death. We fear what others may say or think of us. Some will tell you that fear motivates them. Personally, I would hate to live a life where fear is my primary motivator. True, fear can help you to avoid danger, which is good, but we don't want to rely on fear as a motivator for our most meaningful life accomplishments. If fear is your main motivator, you will find yourself always on the edge. You will be worn out. It isn't sustainable. When people, such as climbers, tell me that they rely on an element of fear, I think they are probably referring to their reaction to fear, which is adrenaline.

For climbers, just as for us all, when we can see our fears in front of us, we get a rush when we begin tackling the fear, and another rush when we defeat it. The reaction to acting despite fear is the body obeying your willpower and giving you the energy to act. That isn't fear; that is courage. It is the lifeblood of accomplishment.

One can choose to go back toward safety or forward toward growth. Growth must be chosen again and again; fear must be overcome again and again. —ABRAHAM MASLOW

THE WORST-CASE SCENARIO

Some people swear by fear as a motivator, but for most of us, focusing on what may go wrong or what you cannot do blocks you from success. However, focusing on what can go wrong is not the same as planning for worst-case scenarios. Focusing on bad outcomes is negative thinking; planning for bad outcomes is just smart strategy.

When I was in the military, we used to say that you are allowed to consider what might go wrong, but that's not where your main focus of attention should be. In the preparatory stages of an exercise, we often asked the question "What if," in order to promote our security. In battle, having planned for worst-case scenarios can mean the difference between life and death. To feel confident in success and to be assured of survival, we had to know what could go wrong.

Both in business and in sports, people forget to prepare for the worst-case scenario. Usually we are aware of potentially bad outcomes; often we can't stop thinking about them; rarely do we do anything about them. It is impossible to avoid thinking about how something can go wrong, but it is possible to control these thoughts and make them work for us.

Most of the things we worry about are actually healthy concerns. It is just our undirected worrying that is bad. When we don't control our human tendency to imagine outcomes, we create negative thoughts that can become chaotic and frequent. They paralyze and hinder us, and we become insecure. This usually happens in the preparatory phases of a task. We size up what needs to be done, and then we immediately begin to recognize pitfalls and hurdles ahead. We begin to worry, and the worry robs our energy from us.

As an athlete, it's essential to have considered the various scenarios that might interfere with the success of your performance. What if the match is rescheduled for one hour earlier than planned? What if the referee is unfair? What if the noise in the arena is deafening? What if I get a bad start, and what if the weather conditions are not on my side? A corporate manager has similar concerns. What if the market suddenly takes a nosedive? What if my competitors release improved products? What if I get bad publicity, what if my best employees resign, and what if I get off on the wrong foot at the important meeting next week?

Twenty percent of my trainings are about rehearsing worst-case scenarios, while the remaining 80 percent is focused on working toward success. Often, clients have this flipped, and spend 80 percent of their energy on how bad everything can go, and hold on to a hope for success with only 20 percent of their energy. That is a surefire recipe for frequent failure.

If most of your attention is focused on the outcome you want, it's much more likely you will actually succeed in achieving it. Success starts in your mind. If you let it, your mind will naturally plop onto the couch and flip through the channels of failure. You know this. You have been in this failure loop before. The longer you sit on the couch, the harder it becomes to do something as simple as push the off button with your finger, get up, and do something else. With your mind, you must do the same thing. You have to force yourself not to watch the endless images of failure. You must force yourself to think about how things can go well and then believe they will go well.

Understanding negative outcome visualization will guide you to plan for the possibility of failure, but more important, it will help you to feel confident in your plan for success. It will help increase the probability of reaching your desired results every hour of the day. This demands practice. You actually have to force your thoughts into the desired direction. You make a choice about what you will think. You are in control of your mind.

Never, never, never give up. —WINSTON CHURCHILL

PRACTICE PATIENCE

Don't forget that you have forces inside you that are much stronger than you can imagine. Those who dare to believe this truth are the ones who succeed. There are countless examples of people who have dared to stand up and face their fears and who have vanquished them. They have focused their attention on the goal far ahead and not on all that could go wrong along the way.

Let yourself be inspired by these stories, both of the famous individuals and of those people you may also find among your own social circle.

This is the key factor of my philosophy. If you don't remind yourself of your goal, you inevitably will be pulled back into your comfort zone. Many people may find enough motivation in simply doing a good job in the present moment, but there is so much more of a rush in looking further up the road. Looking ahead and understanding what you are working toward is essential to always maintaining that little extra desire to choose success in the long run.

But you do not get to your long-term goals without failing along the way. The difficulty is to remember that short-term failure does not spell the failure of your long-term goal. Failing now does not mean failing forever. Often, we have to go through failure in order to learn how to become successful. Learning is never easy. Nothing worthwhile is easy. When you have failed enough times, when things are at their hardest, or when you have been trying too hard for too long, the most difficult thing to do is not give up.

People will tell you that you need to be more persevering. They will tell you to just man up and get it done. But, what all of these common words of advice neglect to acknowledge is an attribute we have largely forgotten in today's world. You must have patience to succeed.

Patience can seem antithetical to success; it isn't. When so many success stories focus on aggressive attributes such as assertiveness or decisiveness, patience is often overlooked. Patience gets a bad rap. Most of us are told to be patient when we have to wait for something we want right now. That isn't patience at all. Patience is not just waiting.

Many people can't be patient for long enough to make the most out of their potential. Those who manage to keep their focus for, say, ten years will experience a sort of exponential development in their career, meaning that what was cumbersome and demanding earlier on gets easier over time. Whereas they once spent four days of work to achieve a decent result, they now spend two workdays and achieve a brilliant result. This sort of effect—in which you achieve better results with less work, or get more done with the same amount of work—requires patience and continued focus over a long period of time.

If you have been a good and hardworking broker for five years, it's likely that the next five years will be easier for you in many ways, because you've already assembled the network and the knowledge you need. The same goes for someone who is writing a dissertation, or someone who is building a company. After a certain amount of time, you start to see connections and can make use of synergies that make any subsequent work both simpler and more enjoyable. When I studied to earn a master's degree in economics and business, I experienced the last year of my studies as much more rewarding and enjoyable than the first.

Many of the very rich have made their fortunes after the age of fifty. Maybe you will be able to reap the fruits of all of your competence only during the very last years of your career. In that case, your patience will be rewarded, because a good many give up along the way. As you are reading this you might be thinking that you can't wait. You want success now. Success begins now. It is not something that suddenly comes and goes. It is a lifestyle that can pay off with great financial reward, if you live it well enough. Patience begins now as well. It isn't something you use here and there. Patience is living successfully one day at a time, giving it your all again and again until your all becomes bigger and better.

Both success and patience are slow burners. If you practice both, starting today, you will find that competitors cannot keep up with your speed, and you will stand out with a unique expertise honed over time. The capacity for long-term thinking and for delayed gratification can be hugely valuable in all areas of life.

THE SLEEPLESS NIGHT

Without a doubt, the Thursday all-nighter is the component of Hell Week that inspires the most doubt in people. Sleep is the great solace in so many lives, a blissful reprieve from the energy-sapping chaos of the modern world. Why on earth would anyone want to deny him- or herself, even just for a night? Of course, that's exactly the point. Forgoing sleep is the ultimate departure from our comfort zone.

Before I go any further, let me stress that you should consider completing this challenge only if it won't put you or others in harm's way. If you operate heavy machinery for a living or have a long commute by car to work, the sleepless night isn't advisable. Or if you have a medical condition that's exacerbated by fatigue, skip the challenge. But for the average healthy adult, missing a single night's sleep shouldn't pose any danger. (By the way, the most widely cited record for staying awake is 264 hours, attained by a seventeen-year-old high school student from California back in 1964.)

So assuming it's safe for you to stay up all night, the next question is: Can you do it? Your gut response is probably *No way!* You need to get past that knee-jerk response and really ask yourself *Can I do it?* The answer is that you can. As with every aspect of Hell Week, you need to prepare. For starters, you should deploy the lessons from Wednesday's time management and map out the night, down to the very minute. If it's just you staring at the clock in a deathly quiet house, you won't stand a chance. Specific tasks will help pass the time. Try to make one of these tasks fairly substantial—a major assignment from work that needs finishing, for example, or an art project that you haven't been able to get off the ground. I've had many clients use the opportunity to catch up on correspondence, in some cases writing people they lost touch with years ago. I think you'll find you're in the right mind-set for that kind of action. There's something about being awake in the middle of the night while the rest of the world sleeps that puts people in a contemplative mood.

I'm also not opposed to you tackling this challenge with another person. I've often coached teams through Hell Week, including the editorial staff at a newspaper and the sales division at an apparel company. In that kind of collective Hell

Week, participants might form groups of two or three for Thursday night and spend a good chunk of the evening on a specific work project. This makes for a different kind of experience, more bonding than introspective, but in the end it meets the same goal of getting each individual outside of his or her comfort zone.

DAVE'S STORY

We have these meet-and-greet events at work, a chance to introduce yourself to all the new hires in the organization. They're a little bit awkward, and I'm not the most extroverted guy in the world, so I usually avoid them. But I forced myself to go to one this week, to get out of my comfort zone. It definitely was awkward in the beginning, but I eventually struck up a conversation with a few new colleagues, all of whom were smart and interesting. I even ended up talking for a while with the head of HR. I didn't seek her out in the crowd or anything. We just ended up standing next to each other. I think it probably made a positive impression on her, which only helps my standing in the organization. It made me realize that when you put yourself out there, good things happen.

JILLIAN'S STORY

I think what I'm realizing is that my comfort zone doesn't really invite other people in. I'm most comfortable when I'm in my own little bubble. I'm pretty introverted by nature, so it makes sense. And I'm not about to start being a Chatty Cathy at the office, inviting people to lunch and setting up weekend retreats. But I have opened up a little bit more with people since starting this process, and it's been mostly positive. In particular, I've made an effort to connect with a few colleagues who I can tell are like me—you know, a little guarded and reserved. I could tell they were unsure of my motive, but once we got past that initial awkwardness, we ended up having a nice conversation. I don't think we're going to become besties, but it felt good to make the human connection.

ADAM'S STORY

Eating is the ultimate for me, so getting outside of the comfort zone is pretty easy. Just stop eating. It has been pretty hard, especially being in a bad mood most of the time. But I have been able to recognize that tucking into a burger and fries or a bag of potato chips would be a short-term solution for my crankiness. A couple hours later I'd be right back where I started. Whereas the good feeling I've had from exercise lasts longer. I'm miserable when it's happening, but then I feel good for a while after. With eating, it's the opposite. I feel good shoveling food in my mouth, but then I feel like crap.

FRIDAY: REST AND RESTITUTION

At this point in the week, there should be no doubt in your mind about why this is called Hell Week. If you've done it right, it's been a tough week, maybe the toughest week you can remember. You should feel mentally and physically exhausted. You should also feel great—the satisfaction that comes with good, honest hard work.

You should also feel different, changed from who you were before you began. If you don't, it might simply be because you have not had time to reflect over the week. Once you reflect, you will begin to realize how much your choice to pursue Hell Week has done for you. You have changed because you chose to. Exactly how you've changed is up to you. Only you can accurately determine how you are different, which is why you must listen to yourself. Reflection is something that you must take time for. It is a natural human process, but we tend to push it away a lot because it requires a certain level of peace and quiet to reflect properly. Peace and quiet is a precious commodity in today's world.

Often, the only time we reflect during the day is right before we go to sleep. This is because your mind is not occupied with tasks and your body is inactive. You are lying still; all you can do is either fall asleep or think—and often that thinking turns into reflection. I probably don't need to tell you that late-night reflection is usually not very healthy. You end up thinking about things that worry you. As a result, you don't sleep well. To avoid this, you need to set aside time to rest, so you can process your thoughts peacefully instead of restlessly.

Friday is rest day. On Thursday, I told you that you should only take the easy road in life when you have pushed yourself and deserve a reward. Friday is a kind of reward, but don't look at it as a day to waste. Everything about Friday is meaningful. Rest is not downtime. Rest can and should be a meaningful exercise, an exercise that augments the effects of more strenuous work.

To begin your reflection period on Hell Week, I will make several suggestions. You are free to replace them with activities that help you relax better. The critical thing is that you rest with purpose.

A FRESH START

When you complete Thursday of Hell Week at 5:00 a.m. on Friday, having been up for a full twenty-four hours, I suggest you take a long, hot shower, preferably finishing off with ice-cold water for the last ten to twenty seconds to jump-start your system, and then eat a healthy breakfast. This morning you can drop exercise and postpone it until evening. But if you're really tired, it can be a good idea to exercise.

Exercise wakes you up. It gives you energy more than it

depletes it. So you have to make a tough decision: exercise or no exercise; it is up to you. Remember, today you will have to go to work as usual and take part in all the activities you would normally participate in. The only difference between this Friday and other Fridays is that you haven't slept the night before. And so you need to be wide awake and grab any chances you get for brief and effective rest.

During the short spaces of reflection throughout the day, ask yourself what Hell Week has meant to you so far. Think about how you felt before the week began. Ask yourself how you felt each day. Ask yourself how you feel today. Finally, ask yourself how you might feel tomorrow. Asking yourself these questions and answering them, honestly and fully and only to yourself, will process your feelings. It will make you conscious of who you are, what you can do, and what lies ahead. It makes you stronger. Going through Hell Week without reflecting is like going to work but not cashing your paycheck. Reflect. It pays.

THE POWER OF REST

I'll now share what my years as a mental trainer have taught me about rest. After that, I'll introduce you to a selection of rest techniques that have proven effective with many of my clients.

Rest is the period to gather strength and energy. It's when you recharge your batteries and recuperate. While we all know that sleep is necessary, we often view rest as a luxury, when in fact it is a necessary part of successful living. The beneficial effect of rest is that it makes you more creative and helps you learn more rapidly. Rest gives you energy, perspective, and the power to deal with matters more efficiently and with greater vigor.

While the benefits of rest are more or less the same for all of us, rest is still highly individual, and it is up to you to determine your proper rest routine. Research is constantly telling us new things about the science of rest. One of the best things you can do is to listen to your body and adapt your rest routine accordingly. Sometimes you will want to rest when your body doesn't really need it, and sometimes your body will need rest when you are too busy to listen. Mess with your rest for long enough, and it will start messing back.

Rest is a critical area for me to cover as a mental trainer in my daily conversations with clients. With rest, as with many issues, most people fall into one of two camps—those who do too much and those who do too little.

CAMP ONE: THE OVER-RESTERS

Camp one includes people who get too much rest. Symptoms of this group are that you sleep in on a regular basis. You take naps when you don't need them. You end up binge watching your favorite TV series when you should be checking off your to-do list. You waste hours on Facebook instead of answering emails. You reward yourself with breaks, not because you earned them, but because you are avoiding the task at hand. If you nodded yes to any of these things, you are in camp one. Do not despair, though. If you have the courage to admit you are in this group, you are already on your way out of it.

It is simple to say that over-resters simply need to stop sleeping and lazing around so much, but there is more to it than that. This group has a fundamental misunderstanding about what rest is and how it works. If excessive rest were a simple problem, it would be easily remedied by just resting less. But that treatment is not enough, because resting too much is only part of the reason why camp one abuses the resource of rest.

Rest is an instrument, and like any instrument, rest is only as good as the skill of its user. The best litmus test for your skill level is your motivation for rest. If you are using rest to avoid dealing with obstacles between you and your goals, then your skill level is low. The only way to remedy this problem is to re-calibrate your motivation for rest. You have to begin resting for the right reasons. If you do this, you will find that the ailments of camp one—feelings of laziness, apathy, and listlessness—begin to diminish and the true benefits of rest will begin to activate.

CAMP TWO: THE UNDER-RESTERS

Others never get enough rest; they are in camp two. They work too hard and don't manage to prioritize their time properly. If you are an under-rester, consider why you undervalue rest. Do you get to bed late and get up early to get work done? Do you work through your lunch break? Do you order takeout, because you don't have time to cook a meal? Is your weekend indistinguishable from your weekdays, because you just have too much to get done? If you are in camp two, you are probably guilty of a few of these. And to make matters worse, you are probably proud of it.

When was the last time you took a vacation? If you are in this camp, it has probably been too long. You lack faith in rest.

You do not trust that it is as inherently valuable as the things you are choosing to replace rest with. Neglecting rest is bankrupting your success. It is taking an energy loan that you can never pay back.

Interestingly, the results of camp one and camp two are strikingly similar. Both groups are low on energy. When you rest too much, you end up becoming lethargic. When you rest too little, you are running on an empty tank. Both inactivity and overactivity are sources of stress and tension. Both will leave you feeling dissatisfied with life and unsuccessful. The sweet spot, where you feel energized, productive, and rested, is the balance both camps must move toward, if they want success. As Hell Week has shown you, neglecting rest in order to push through and complete hard tasks is sometimes necessary, but when you consistently neglect rest, you and your work will inevitably suffer.

Like camp one, camp two has a fundamental misunderstanding about what rest is. Under-resters view rest as a necessary physical function like going to the bathroom, and so camp two rests only when the need is as demanding as a bathroom visit.

Many of us undervalue rest as a useless time-waster. And having come this far in Hell Week, you may think that rest contradicts the essence of my philosophy of hard work. But rest and hard work are inexorably linked. The best of the best rest more thoroughly, and more consciously, than others. It's always striking to me how many of the really excellent clients I work with, the truly world-class ones, are expert resters. They are driven by what they do and manage the impossible—that is, to feel good about themselves, to have control, to accomplish everything they desire, and at the same time feel in harmony with themselves and their surroundings. If you look at people at the top of any field, you will find it conspicuous how many of them don't stress, don't complain, and don't have a chaotic daily life. What keeps their high-octane lives glued together? Proper and adequate rest.

Activity and rest are two vital aspects of life. To find a balance in them is a skill in itself. Wisdom is knowing when to have rest, when to have activity, and how much of each to have. Finding them in each other—activity in rest and rest in activity—is the ultimate freedom. —SRI SRI RAVI SHANKAR

FINDING THAT SWEET SPOT

I think back here to my own military Hell Week in 1992. As part of the mental training regimen, we were required to learn vocabulary in a foreign language as well as the names of various classical music compositions, while at the same time completing intense physical challenges. It was amazing how difficult it was to learn even the most basic concepts as our rest periods decreased.

For most people, more rest will mean better results in every area of their lives. But it is important to remember that rest has to be planned. It has to become part of your daily routine, your week, your month, and your year. *Consciousness* is a key word in mental training, and rest must also be something you do consciously. Rest must become a deliberate part of your life.

How should you rest during a day, a week, a month, or a year? There is no simple solution. How long your vacations should be, and how many weekends off you should take, are things you have to discover for yourself. On a general level, I believe many people take too much time off, and also cannot fully appreciate vacations because they have not worked hard enough leading up to them. In addition, they lose the pleasure that comes from working hard over a period of time. We should not just work with a restful vacation in mind. We should be consciously finding rest in the peace of mind hard work provides. Far too many people do something somewhere in between. Most people get on well in life. Most people perform well. Most people perform in their jobs passably well and find reasonable enjoyment in their vacations. Your challenge is to not be like most people. Your challenge is to do everything fully. Work fully. Rest fully.

I believe from time to time in life you really need to step on the accelerator, and at other times strive for an increased sense of calm and balance. As we have discussed, we must choose areas of focus to be effective. I believe that during a month you can spend a week focusing on your work, and at other periods emphasize other values and activities. Think both long range and short term, and cast your mind back to time management, mood, and focus. Hell Week should help you to discover where your limits lie. Considering these things should help you to discover how rest will accompany your workweek and life goals.

During Hell Week you must go to bed at 10:00 p.m. and get up at 5:00 a.m. This should be enough sleep. If in addition you build in different kinds of rest during the day, especially on Hell Week's Friday, you can quite easily be on your feet and working hard throughout the day. I think seven to eight hours is enough for most people with a fairly average day. During

Hell Week you should fall asleep more rapidly, because surfing online has to be kept to a minimum and TV of course is not allowed at all.

A change is as good as a rest. —STEPHEN KING

THE REST OF VARIETY

Rest exists in many forms. Beyond actual sleep, it can be meditation, a hot bath, time with loved ones, or even work. Yes, work can be a form of rest as well. Take a look at your to-do list. Find the item that is the hardest task on your list and imagine that you have begun working on it. You likely consider this your hardest task because you aren't quite sure how to solve it. It will require a lot of thinking, juggling, and patience. Now imagine that after making some headway in this task, you decide to spend some time knocking out some of your easier tasks. Look at the easiest task on your list. Imagine yourself leaving the difficult task and taking a break by working on the easy task. Doesn't that feel like a break to you?

It can be a kind of rest to do something completely different. The key is that you cannot keep thinking about the previous task while working on the new one. If you do that, then you aren't resting, you are just wearing yourself thin. I'll give you an example. If you're one of the many people who have a job that starts at around 9:00 a.m. and finish your working day at around 5:00 p.m. or later, then usually you come home feeling exhausted. If your job is very involved, then it's not unusual to take work thoughts home with you. This is a huge mistake and should be avoided. It doesn't benefit you to be partly present at home and partly thinking about work. If you develop this debilitating habit, you will find that you are never fully anywhere.

You will begin to recharge your batteries more efficiently if you think of the stairs leading up to the door at home or the elevator up to your apartment as magical—a magical stairway that makes all your thoughts about work disappear. You switch off your cell phone on the way home, and it should remain switched off for at least an hour because you want to wind down and recuperate when you come home. You want to rest by shifting your thoughts. You have the ability within you if you want to do it.

What you do at home for the first hour is irrelevant, as long as you do it 100 percent with your thoughts 100 percent present in what you are doing. Perhaps you spend time with your significant other. Perhaps you have dinner with your children or with friends. Be inquisitive about the people around you, be attentive, and be at your best in this role.

The magic stairway or elevator is so magical that it makes you shift focus, and that gives you energy. Tell yourself you're totally on the ball, you're now going to be the best parent in the world, or you're going to be at your best as a spouse or partner. On your way into the magical sphere, undergo a change, because you have control over your own thoughts. Imagine yourself doing this as you make your way to work. Imagine coming home and being first class in your role at home. It has to be wholehearted. In this way, you will manage to give something to the people around you, and this will benefit you at work, as well. You are able to step on the gas during longer working days as required, producing better quality in what you're doing and improving your performance. You might ask why this is considered resting advice, but once you experience the satis-fying feeling of knowing you are in the moment and living life fully, you will answer that question for yourself.

Doing something different purely and simply is a kind of rest. It produces an effect similar to taking a weekend off or going on vacation.

WHY AND HOW TO MEDITATE

I am a big believer in the restorative power of meditation. Not only does it bring mental clarity and acuity, it makes the body stronger and healthier. Indeed, clients who begin regular meditation tell me they get sick far less frequently.

In addition to having a good night's sleep, taking breaks for meditation can be an incredibly effective form of rest, especially if you have spells of broken sleep during the night. We're already seeing more Western companies offer collective meditation sessions for employees throughout the day to increase productivity. On Hell Week's Friday, I want you to try it out several times throughout the day.

The goal is to reach a meditative state in which you're neither asleep nor awake. Meditation experts talk about scales of consciousness. At the top of the scale is "wide awake," at the bottom "deep sleep." Between the two extremes are other levels. Imagine you're in a deep sleep before being awakened by a slamming door caused by the wind. As you sink back down into sleep, there will be a moment where you're suspended between the two levels. This is the meditative state.

When I took my first course in meditation, I became aware of these levels. There is something remarkable about them, the way a person, with proper training and technique, can actually move into a level and stay there without progressing further. In that state, you become balanced and calm, your mind clears, and your body experiences absolute rest.

As I got more into meditation, I was amazed to learn how many hugely successful people are practitioners— though I shouldn't have been surprised. The who's who of meditators includes names like Bill Clinton, Oprah Winfrey, Clint Eastwood, Tina Turner, David Lynch, Arianna Huffington, and George Lucas. Sigmund Freud and Winston Churchill used their own forms of meditation, as did Leonardo da Vinci, who reportedly meditated to manage his work with increasing efficiency throughout his life.

While I strongly recommend taking a proper course on meditation, below are a couple of exercises you can try on Friday. They're not meditation per se, but they serve a similar purpose. And you can do them anywhere—on a bus, in a parked car, at the office, or in the comfort of home. Try to find somewhere you won't be disturbed, and do one of the exercises at least every other hour on Friday, spending five to ten minutes each time. Ideally, you should be seated comfortably in a chair during both exercises, without leaning your head back on a headrest.

Exercise One: The Keys Meditation Method

Take out a set of keys and hold it in your hand in such a way that when you drop it, it will fall to the floor. Close your eyes. Take three deep breaths, in through your nose and out through your mouth. Feel yourself relax. Isolate one group of muscles at a time and feel them relax. Breathe normally. Try to fall asleep. As you enter the level where you lose control of your body, you will drop the keys, ending the exercise. You'll have had a perfect short break that will ensure you're better prepared to continue the day's tasks with full focus and extreme efficiency. This is an effective "power nap," in which you move relatively quickly through several levels of sleep.

Exercise Two: Bertrand's Little Rest

Sit as comfortably as you can, planting the soles of your feet on the floor. Let your hands lie loosely on your lap. Close your eyes. Breathe in and out deeply three times.

Do as you did in the previous exercise, going through all the parts of your body and muscle groups. Think about your feet. Envisage them inside your shoes and socks, and see that they are relaxed completely. Your legs and thighs, feel that they are totally at ease and check if they can become even more relaxed. Your diaphragm should go in and out with your breath. Make sure your jaw muscles and the muscles elsewhere in your body are relaxed.

Breathe in and out three times. What do you hear? For about one minute, you should be extremely focused on what you hear. What sounds are there around you? Can you manage to distinguish one sound from another? Can you hear your breath? Can you hear your heartbeat? Do you hear any sounds from a distance? What do you smell? For about one minute, you should be extremely focused on what you smell. What smells are there around you right now? Can you distinguish one from another? Can you smell your own scent? What do you taste? For about one minute, you should try to identify what taste you have in your mouth. What did you eat last? Can you still taste it? Are there different tastes on different parts of your tongue?

Think of a situation when you were happy. For three to five minutes you should be in that situation. It may be a long time ago, or quite recently. Where were you? What did you see? What did you hear? Immerse yourself in the situation as best you can. What did you feel? What did you notice? What did you do? What were you thinking? Concentrate on your breathing for about one minute. Follow your breath in through your nose, down your windpipe, and deep down into your lungs. Follow it out again. Imagine you have a camera following the progress of your breath as it goes in and out. For two to three minutes, you will imagine your life in your dreams. Imagine that you have realized one or several of your great goals. Use all your senses and see yourself being successful. Feel what it's like to obtain what you deserve. For one final minute, try to simply be. Empty your head. Take a peek at your watch, because you should spend a maximum of twenty minutes total on this exercise.

DAVE'S STORY

The improvement in my sleep is one of the biggest ways I've benefited from Hell Week. For years, I've been in the habit of watching TV on the computer for an hour or so before going to bed. Ahead of Hell Week, I bought a big, fat novel that I've been reading every night. I don't think I got through more than ten pages before falling fast asleep. There was one night where I nodded off before 9:00 p.m. and slept straight through until 5:00 a.m. That hasn't happened in a long, long time. I've been so much more alert as a result and my energy level has been higher.

I also tried the Keys Meditation Method a few times throughout the week. I'm not sure it worked completely, but I did feel refreshed afterward. They've started offering midday meditation classes at my work. I never considered them before, but now I'm definitely going to give them a try.

JILLIAN'S STORY

Late nights sort of come with the territory in my work, so I can't say I was in bed every night at 10:00 p.m. But I did get more sleep than I'm used to, and definitely noticed an improvement in my ability to focus and concentrate. I haven't taken the plunge into meditation yet, but I feel like I can't open a magazine or newspaper without hearing some mention of it, so I guess I better give it a try.

ADAM'S STORY

I never realized the connection between sleep and food. There are a lot of times when I'll stay up watching TV or something, and sooner or later I'll end up heading to the fridge or pantry. The whole midnight-snack routine. So being in bed at 10:00 p.m. this week has taken that out of the equation. And it's not like I've gone to bed hungry, because I've shifted the whole pattern around. I think all those hours when I haven't been productive, when I've been a little bored, are where my worst eating habits started. If I can work on being a more deliberate sleeper and rester, it will take away one more source of mindless eating.

SATURDAY: CONTROLLING YOUR INNER DIALOGUE

You have now put five-sevenths of Bertrand's Hell Week behind you. Since the two previous days have taken you to the extreme both physically and mentally, the two final days are gentler. You are over the worst, but the two remaining days are still demanding, and they will be most rewarding if you take the task seriously.

You awake on Saturday morning at 5:00 as usual, well rested after seven hours of restorative sleep. After your sleepless Thursday night, I assume you fell asleep the moment your head hit the pillow Friday night. Remember that you are going to work this Saturday.

Thursday was an experiment in pushing yourself, despite lack of sleep, and doing a lot of what you had previously postponed. Saturday will be an experiment of a slightly different character. Saturday is intended to be a so-called "happy day." If this sounds a little cheesy or overly earnest to you, it is because the world has largely come to undervalue simple happiness. Saturday will help you to remember that happiness is not all that complex. At least it doesn't need to be, if we don't make it that way. Saturday should be a day where you decide to think exclusively positive and assertive thoughts about the world and the people around you, but first and foremost about yourself.

My aim with this day is for you to experience the enormous importance of your own way of thinking in shaping how you feel. When you do more of the right activities, with a positive attitude, you will find it has a self-reinforcing effect. With good feelings, good actions follow. Good actions, in turn, increase your feelings of achievement and recognition. If you are conscious of what you say to yourself, if you train yourself to steer your thoughts in your desired direction of action, you will also to a large degree learn to steer your feelings as well. Obviously not everyone's mood can be controlled with the power of positive thinking. For example, serious illnesses such as clinical depression can require medication. Still, many of us can take ownership of our emotional life and begin to steer it in a more positive direction.

Many people have a tendency to think themselves down. Today you're going to regard it as your task to do the exact opposite of that. At the outset this is a difficult task, because many of us have programmed our minds to think negatively for decades. The Saturday of Hell Week should be an experiment in positivity. Remember that experiments can take many attempts, so don't give up when your thoughts get the better of you. Pick yourself up, dust yourself off, and grapple with your thoughts again. No thoughts are too powerful to keep you down forever.

Because you will be battling your natural tendency to think negatively, do not try to rein yourself in if you feel you are becoming excessively praising, positive, and optimistic toward yourself. Don't concern yourself with being realistic. It is better to shoot past your target with this exercise than to fall short. This is not an exercise in realism. If you are particularly rational, and want to see the sensible, the logical, or the scientific aspects of every circumstance, you will probably find this a greater challenge than many others. But don't let that be your excuse. Succeed anyway.

A pessimist sees the difficulty in every opportunity; an optimist sees the opportunity in every difficulty. —WINSTON CHURCHILL

INNER DIALOGUE

Human beings never stop thinking. This is our blessing and our curse. Sometimes we think smart, constructive, solution-oriented, positive, and appropriate thoughts about the situations we find ourselves in, but at other times, we do exactly the opposite. You can probably think of numerous situations, especially with the benefit of hindsight, where you could have thought more positive thoughts. You can probably also go a step further and see how the situation would have been improved if you had used positive thinking. Some people are exceptionally conscious of this way of thinking. Most of us are not.

Most of the time, our thoughts drone on in an endless stream of words. Some thoughts are conscious, others subconscious, and others somewhere in between. When we try to grasp the entirety of our thought patterns and imagine trying to control them, we can easily become intimidated. Focusing on that feeling of intimidation is a negative thought. Recognizing it but then telling yourself that you don't need to control everything, you only need to start somewhere and control some thoughts, is positive thinking.

Inner dialogue is that endless conversation all people conduct within their minds, every day, every minute, from the moment they wake in the morning until they fall asleep at night. If you teach yourself to become more aware of this dialogue, to steer it and manipulate it, you will be able to improve your performance dramatically, and you will feel increased degrees of happiness more often. To achieve this demands high levels of awareness, and the battle begins as soon as the alarm clock rings in the morning.

I recently ended a Skype session with my own personal coach, an amazingly capable woman with whom I can have verbal jousts about everything between heaven and earth. Even a mental trainer like myself needs an energizing boost from time to time, and this was such a moment. We talked about my past, and I told her about my dreams, goals, and visions. I was very frank, and added that "Yes, I'm extremely pleased with, even proud of, what I've achieved as a mental trainer during the past few years in Norway. The rational part of me that looks at the facts tells me I've had lots of brilliant results. But when I dream of my life ten years from now, I hear an internal voice saying: *Erik, you've got too high an opinion of yourself now. What if you don't manage it—think how disappointed you'll be. Erik, you haven't got what it takes to succeed. Be satisfied with what you've managed and try to maintain the level you're at now.*"

When I related these thoughts to my coach, she said, "What

about taking a few days of not allowing that voice in your head to speak. Let it be nonexistent for a while. Because deep inside, you know you're going to give your biggest dreams a go anyway. And you know that if you try, then there's a big difference between trying with the belief that it might go well, and trying while believing you won't just try, you'll really put your fantasies into action, and they will go brilliantly."

She said what I usually say to my own clients: you choose what to say to yourself mentally, and that affects your beliefs, emotions, and actions. A goal is a dream that can seem too big, difficult, demanding, and perhaps even impossible to attain. For many people, this is linked with such great fear that they don't even try to reach it. I tell myself that I will be proud regardless of the outcome, and then I give it everything I have.

FINDING THE FEEL-GOOD FACTOR

The feel-good factor I experience by believing that dreams and goals, great and small, are going to be fulfilled is just as all-encompassing as the feeling I get if I imagine things not going well. The battle between these two can be difficult and discouraging. Many people decide to just give up and allow themselves to be negative thinkers, losing out on a much higher level of success because of it. I experience the feel-good factor by thinking that in ten years, I will be thinking, *Yes, I did it!* rather than thinking, *It didn't work, but I'm so proud I gave it my best shot.* But if I end up thinking the latter of the two, I will still be happy, because I tried and I believed in myself.

It's not necessarily the moment when you realize you've succeeded that's the most important. Trite but true, the journey is what counts. When my coach asked me to shut out my negative thoughts, and then to observe what effect it had on me, I knew as she spoke that she was right. I knew it would be productive to block out my negative thoughts. If, after my best efforts, my negative thoughts still popped up, then I would quickly swap them with positive ones, such as *It's going to be just fine*.

If you think often enough that everything's going to turn out well, then you eventually come to believe this so strongly that all doubt is removed. Yes, it is a form of conditioning, a type of programming, and maybe even a kind of brainwashing. But you are the one choosing to change; nobody is making you do it. Wouldn't it be wonderful to go through life with a more positive and optimistic attitude?

THE THINKING BEING

We are thinking, reflecting beings, and this is the very thing that distinguishes us from other species. We have the ability to judge, analyze, and think logically and precisely. We can use our imaginations. We can be creative and intuitive. We can see the big picture and understand things abstractly. We can think in an array of different ways. We have the ability to look back in time, as well as think of the present and the future. We are able to think rationally, find information, and remember precise facts that we have learned. We can summon up associations, and we can call upon an enormous repertoire of emotions. We can understand connections.

With all these faculties of thought, we have the ability to place our lives in perspective. Doing so in this context involves reflection. That ability is something only human beings possess.

The majority of animals live only in the present moment; they have no inner dialogue, they don't reflect on their situation in the world, and they only exist, here and now. Our thought world is so well developed that with a bit of luck and a lot of work, we can teach ourselves to control it. If we simply let our thoughts flow freely, we won't bring out our potential. Think about what limiting thoughts we often choose to think, a tendency that again affects not only the outcome but how we actually feel about ourselves along the way.

WORD CHOICE

The words you use also affect your feelings. Your feelings affect your behavior, and they in turn are crucial to whether you make a right or wrong decision. Words can provide equally powerful associations as, for example, images, sounds, or smells. If you're aware of which pieces of music, film clips on YouTube, and images make you feel motivated, then you can make them accessible and use them every time you feel the need. If you're aware of which people build you up and make you feel better, and make a point of spending more time with them, then that will have a positive effect. That's how it is with the language we use, as well. A simple word can signify a little or a lot. But a word you speak aloud, or say to yourself, can be just what's required to adjust your mood slightly there and then.

Words create associations. The verb *to hope* suggests that you are putting your trust in something other than yourself. To hope is to depend on some external factor to ensure things will go well. While hope can be a powerful emotion, it is also often a word we use as a shield from actually having to accept our own responsibility for an outcome. This kind of hoping means you are not sure. Hoping does not mean security and a conviction that you have what it takes to deliver. So using the word *hope* during your preparations means you are giving up before you get started.

Immediately before a difficult moment you have prepared for, you have to switch hope with: "I'm absolutely positive, I'm secure because I have prepared, I'm feeling all systems go because . . ." If you add an extra dose of assertiveness to your state of mind, then the uncertainty associated with hope will be pushed aside. If you truly desire success in your life, you will make words work for you. After all, both negative and positive thoughts are composed of words, so why not choose the right ones and reap the benefit?

Saturday of Hell Week deals with a lot of abstracts, I know. But they all boil down to one thing: taking charge of your inner dialogue and keeping it pointed in a positive direction. For one day, the negative voices will be banished and you will see life for all its brilliant possibilities.

Adam's Story

There are a lot of competing voices in my head. But I think the biggest discovery I've made is that when it comes to eating, and maybe some of the other addictions in my life, it's more about the voice that's not in my head. Which is to say, so much of the behavior is automatic—just eating or drinking for the sake of eating or drinking. I feel like if I can be more mindful in those moments and force some sort of inner dialogue into the behavior—Why are you eating that? Why are you drinking that?—I might actually be able to get a handle on the situation.

Dave's Story

In my last call with Erik before Hell Week, he told me that my overarching goal for the week was to stay positive. "Super Dave," he called me. I have a lot of negative voices in my head, so it wasn't easy, but I managed to do it. One example: the Monday of Hell Week my father was coming around for dinner. I'd made meatballs the night before, and I'd accidentally added too much salt. My tendency in the past would have been to make a big fuss over the fact, saying "I'm sorry if the meatballs are too salty," etc. Instead, I just served the meal and kept it positive. "Great meatballs," my father said. That's how it went all week long. My positive attitude set the tone for every interaction, and I came away feeling really good about myself.

SUNDAY: PUTTING LIFE INTO PERSPECTIVE

I've always been a bit of a history buff, especially when it comes to the Roman Empire—great characters, epic tales, and endless insights into human nature. As a mental trainer, I particularly like one custom from that epoch that has to do with the Latin expression *memento mori*, which translates into "remember that you will die." According to Roman scholars, the ruling senate would often celebrate army generals returning from a victorious raid with a triumphant parade. This event was considered the highest mark of honor, and no expense would be spared for the general and his men as they were led through streets lined with cheering crowds.

The general himself used to stand atop a gilded chariot, looking down on the teeming masses. There was always a slave behind him, holding the hallmark crown of laurels above the general's head as a sign of victory. The slave served another purpose, however. Every now and then, amid the cheers and roars, he would lean forward and whisper into the general's ear, "*memento mori*." The words were a reminder that, despite the general's great and heroic victory in battle, he was still a mortal being with limited time on Earth. Today might be a day of celebration. But tomorrow he would have to return to battle and the pursuit of human excellence.

Why am I sharing this story with you now? Because with the end of Hell Week in sight, I believe you've accomplished a major feat. You should certainly feel good about the accomplishment, like the Roman general riding high aboard his chariot. But the end of Hell Week must also be a period of reflection, and there's no better way to do this than by coming face-to-face with your own mortality. Think of me as the slave whispering into your ear.

There are these two young fish swimming along, and they happen to meet an older fish swimming the other way, who nods at them and says, "Morning, boys. How's the water?" And the two young fish swim on for a bit, and then eventually one of them looks over at the other and goes, "What the hell is water?" —DAVID FOSTER WALLACE

THE MOTIVATION OF MORTALITY

As with Saturday, there's little in the way of an actual agenda for this final day of Hell Week. I still expect you to be up at 5:00 a.m. with the same eager approach for the day. Assuming you don't have a job to get to, you might plan a particularly rigorous workout, followed by extended quality time with family or friends. At some point in the day, however, you should definitely carve out some alone time, at least an hour, and preferably two. During this time you will put the events of the week and your life as a whole into perspective.

Without dwelling too heavily on the mortality theme,

I truly believe the finality of life is one of the greatest motivators we have at our disposal. I'll often ponder the fact that, like every other person on the planet, I shall one day die. I actually picture myself in the final moment, as time stops and everything comes to an end. Though I realize it could happen at any time, I do at least grant myself the best-case scenario, one where I'm an old man lying on my deathbed, with a lifetime of experiences behind me. I ask myself, Am I proud of my life? Did I accomplish all that I hoped to accomplish?

It might sound a little melodramatic, but there's nothing negative or ponderous to the fantasy. It's simply a way of imbuing life with a measure of urgency. I once read about an extremely wealthy Norwegian entrepreneur, who supposedly keeps a clock on his computer that's counting down the days, hours, minutes, and seconds left in his life, assuming he lives the average life span. That certainly puts life into perspective. I've found that professional athletes are often good at this as well, given the very finite nature of their careers. Baseball players seldom play past the age of forty. Football players have even shorter runs, while gymnasts and swimmers might be done by the age of twenty. These are the simple realities of their given sports, and it's an excellent motivation for them to be the best they can be while there's time left on the clock.

It can be harder for the rest of us to put life into perspective. As a result, I often end up taking a very hard line with clients on this point. There was the forty-year-old advertising executive who was in a sort of professional paralysis, unable to make the changes needed to move his career and his life forward.

"You can continue on this path for the next two decades," I told him. "But unless you commit to real change, the only thing that will happen is that you'll get older. You'll turn fifty and feel the same way you do today. Then you'll turn sixty and feel the same. All of a sudden you'll be talking about retirement, wondering what the hell happened to the last quarter century of your life."

He started to get the message. A lot of people don't. Think about how much is said and written about the midlife crisis, in blogs and health journals, on talk shows and radio call-ins. Some people laugh it off as a narcissistic construct of the Western world. But I think the crisis is real, and I think it happens not because we're afraid of death but because we refuse to acknowledge its imminence. And so, as a first step toward putting your life into perspective, I want you to embrace mortality.

All those days that came and went,
Little did I know that they were life. —STIG JOHANSSON

FORMALIZE YOUR VALUE SYSTEM

The second task for Sunday, which I believe will bring your life into sharper perspective, is to clearly define your value system. When I meet a client for the first time, I ask a series of simple questions designed to draw this out. Who are you? How would your mother characterize you? How would your friends describe you? What relationships matter most in your life? What are you most proud of? The answers to these questions form a value system. If you've experienced illness, you will probably value health. If you grew up in poverty, wealth and security will likely define your value system. The value system you create will reinforce your behavior. If health is your main value, you will probably eat a healthy diet and exercise on a regular basis. If knowledge is a top value, you will probably become an avid reader and a believer in continuing education.

As you define your value system, it's important to think about how it lines up with your goals. I once had a client who valued economic security above all else. He'd grown up in a single-parent household with a lot of hardship, including time spent in homeless shelters and living on the street. One of his dreams, he told me, was to start his own business. Though I thought his concept for the business was strong, it was in a very volatile industry. As you know, I'm a big proponent of risk, but in this particular instance, it worked so directly against my client's value system that I felt compelled to point out the fact to him. If, on the other hand, wealth had been the foundation of his value system, my advice would have been different. He recognized the dilemma and decided to redirect his goals so that they lined up more directly with his values. He still went on to own and operate a successful business, but he took longer with the launch and chose a lower-risk industry.

Remember, your values map your course in life. They tell you what to do, but also what not to do. At every turn, they'll let you ask yourself, *Is what I'm about to do in accordance with my values?* If the answer is yes, you can go forward. If not, you need to rethink your motives.

LOOK FOR ROLE MODELS AND RIVALS

As a final step toward putting your life into perspective, I want you to spend some time thinking about people you admire and wish to emulate. This is another mental sparring exercise

I do with clients, and it always yields results. "Tell me about someone you look up to," I'll ask them. "Whom do you envy?" Especially if they've already achieved a measure of success in their life, just getting them to admit that there are people out there who've done more than they have can be a challenge. I have to remind them that no matter how accomplished they might be, there will always be someone out there who has done more. And that's a good thing! It means there's always something more to strive for.

Drawing comparisons with other people can be a source of inspiration in other ways. As a child, I used to love reading biographies of famous people like Louis Pasteur, John F. Kennedy, and Thomas Edison. The more I read, the more I realized that many of history's most accomplished people had to overcome huge adversity early in life. Pasteur came from poverty. Kennedy was beset by health problems from an early age. Edison was borderline deaf and, by most accounts, a dreadful student. These revelations encouraged me to rethink my own adversity. Instead of seeing my scrawny build as a source of weakness, it became a challenge. The isolation I experienced in school made me all the more curious about what makes people tick and come together.

Who are the people you relate to most, whether actual contacts in your life, historical figures, or modern-day notables? Understanding what it is about these people that you admire is another great way to direct your energy and thoughts. If there's someone from your industry or line of work who is separating herself from the pack, how has she done it? And what would it take to do the same?

Along with facing your mortality and defining your value

system, identifying role models and rivals will help put your life into perspective. Seeking perspective is an exercise that most people do only at certain times and under certain situations— on New Year's Day, perhaps, or at the start of a new decade in life. There's nothing wrong with that, per se, except that the introspection is somewhat arbitrary. By instead making it the very deliberate end to your Hell Week, I promise you that the perspective you form will be far more meaningful. And it will provide a clear vision for the next vital stage of your life, which I call Life After Hell Week.

ADAM'S STORY

That was hell, just as advertised. But now that it's over, I feel really satisfied. One of my goals going in was to rediscover the athlete I used to be, and I think I succeeded with that. It kind of got my competitive juices going. And I remember the positive feeling that comes when you push yourself just a little bit harder than last time.

JILLIAN'S STORY

I can't sit here and say my life has been completely transformed, but there are some very real takeaways from this experience. I'm seeing many relationships—with colleagues, friends, and family members—in a new light. And I kind of have a different image of myself, if only slightly. I mean, look, it's not like the wheels were falling off my life. But I've come to see that there's even more I can get out of it, though not necessarily by making more money or racking up more accomplishments. I don't know what exactly the alternative goals are yet, but I'm definitely more open to exploring them than I was a week ago.

DAVE'S STORY

I'm feeling better in mind and body after Hell Week than I have in a long time. It's left me believing that when I'm at the top of my game, I can accomplish anything. That's made me reassess my goals in a big way. I have the confidence to aim a lot higher. I'm not exactly sure where that process will lead, but I'm excited to find out.

PART THREE

LIFE AFTER
HELL WEEK

I DO NOT THINK THAT THERE IS ANY OTHER QUALITY SO ESSENTIAL TO SUCCESS OF ANY KIND AS THE QUALITY OF PERSEVERANCE. IT OVERCOMES ALMOST EVERYTHING, EVEN NATURE. —JOHN D. ROCKEFELLER

I'll never forget the end of my first Hell Week. My fellow recruits and I had been in the woods for six straight days, freezing and sleep deprived, pushed to the brink of our physical and mental abilities. For the last forty-eight hours, we'd been lugging 175-pound boxes full of sand, meant to simulate fallen soldiers, over rocky terrain to destinations unknown. We knew that Hell Week must be coming to an end, but when exactly remained a mystery.

Suddenly, the drudgery we were all experiencing was interrupted by the sharp voice of our commanding officer. "Air raid warning!" he screamed. We stopped and looked dumbly at one another. "Dig yourselves in!" the officer barked, which only prompted more blank stares.

Dig myself in? I thought. *How the hell do I do that?* Reading my thoughts, the officer nodded blithely at the shovels we'd been hauling since day one of Hell Week. I'd forgotten all about them. I grabbed a spade and started to hack at the ground, though if you had seen me, you might have called it something else—pecking perhaps, or maybe prodding. I was ailing and exhausted. The shovel felt like a tree trunk in my hands. The most I could manage was a handful of sand with each dig. It was actually kind of fascinating how utterly spent I was, like that moment when you're driving in the car with the fuel gauge pinned on empty, desperate for a gas station, and the car finally conks out.

At last, the officer relented and ordered us to stop. But no sooner was the command out of his mouth than it was followed by another, ordering us to resume marching. I couldn't believe my ears. More marching? Wasn't Hell Week over? We probably marched for another three miles, through a dark forest with thick underbrush that was nearly impossible to step through, so heavy were our legs. Finally we emerged from the shadows of the forest. The officer had us line up.

"Turn to the right," he said. We followed his command and found ourselves suddenly drenched in the warm sunlight. "I wanted you to be back out in the sun," the officer said. This was followed by one of those interminably pregnant pauses that only the military seems to produce. "Hell Week is over," he finally said.

A feeling of intense camaraderie swept through the group. We'd been a much larger group at the start of the process. But then guys dropped out, some by choice, some because they couldn't hack it. The bond between those who remained was as strong as any I'd ever felt. I imagined it was akin to winning an Olympic medal or professional championship in team sports. We felt truly victorious.

A short while later, we were back at camp. I can remember

feeling greatly relieved, but also a sense of anticlimax. Fortunately, I didn't have that long to dwell on it before I was called into the major's office.

I stepped into his quarters and stood firmly at attention, chest out, chin up, heels locked, arms at my sides, hands clenched, and looking straight ahead. This was the moment of truth, where I'd learn if I had earned one of fifty-two spots in the officers' candidate school, out of the original seventeen hundred applicants.

"Major, recruit 39 Larssen!" I said loudly and clearly.

"Sit down," the major said. He gave me a tentative smile before looking down at his papers. "Larssen, your training period has been successful. You were a nobody for the first few weeks. In fact, you were so anonymous that several of the officers didn't know who you were. But during Hell Week, you emerged from the shadows. You're through to the next level. Congratulations."

"Thank you, sir," I replied, while on the inside I let out a ferocious *Yes!*

The next day, we were released for a weekend of R and R. I went home to my mother and father with the greatest sense of satisfaction and accomplishment I'd ever known. My mother had drawn a hot bath that awaited me. The memory of stretching out in the tub is as vivid as the 175-pound box I'd been lugging a few days prior. My exhausted and emaciated body was covered in cuts and bruises. I'd been freezing the better part of the last week. Now I was submerged in steaming hot water. If the woods had been hell, I was now in heaven. I lay there with my eyes shut, basking in the aroma from the hot meal my mother had prepared.

Even today, nearly a quarter century later, I still relive that sensation. It was incredibly pleasant, and it made all the trials and tribulations of the last week well worth it. But more than that, it was a prelude to something new. I was only eighteen years old, and Hell Week was the first real loop in the thread of my young life. It was a high point of achievement and recognition. Never before had I experienced such an extreme departure from my everyday life. It not only made me tougher, it gave me more self-confidence and more security. It was confirmation that just as the officer in survival training had predicted, I could indeed take a lot more than I thought.

I hope your first Hell Week leaves you with a similar feeling. If you followed the program and were 100 percent committed, you should have a real sense of accomplishment (though I hope your body isn't covered in scrapes and bruises!). Your first act should be to reward yourself with the equivalent of a hot bath and warm meal. You might go out to a nice dinner with family or friends, followed by a few episodes of your favorite show. Come Monday morning, sleep until 7:00, if that's what your body wants and your job or family allows. Later in the week, meet friends for drinks. I know I had my share of beers in the days after Hell Week.

But then the time came to return to base for what would amount to an eight-year career in the military. The lessons of Hell Week were with me the entire time, and they are with me today. I hope the same will be true for you. It may not be immediately clear how the experience has changed you. I've had clients contact me six months later to report some new discovery about themselves that they realize had taken root in Hell Week.

I often describe Hell Week and the method behind it as a

holistic approach to self-improvement. It works on your mind and your body, your reason and your emotions, your inner dialogue and the one you have with the outside world. The fact that it's working on so many levels can make its impact hard to untangle. But if you've been involved 100 percent, I assure you the progress is under way. Your goal now is to keep it going. That's what this final section of the book is all about.

Don't worry: no more 5:00 a.m. wake-up calls or militant action plans. However, in the days, weeks, and months after Hell Week, there are some basic steps you should take and questions you should ask yourself to make sure the lessons stick and the momentum is maintained. By now you know that I can't resist structure, so I've divided this process into three parts: one to three months after Hell Week; three to six months after Hell Week; and one year after Hell Week. There's logic to this approach, but it's not meant to be too prescriptive. I simply want the experience of Hell Week to live on—at least until you're ready to go through it again.

ONE TO THREE MONTHS AFTER HELL WEEK

If you're like most of my clients, you probably went into Hell Week thinking it was going to be a constant struggle. I don't doubt that there were some trying moments. Maybe it was the second exercise session of the day toward the end of the week, or the Thursday all-nighter. But most of the people I work with also report on aspects of Hell Week that were easy, and even a lot of fun.

In the immediate aftermath of Hell Week, try to focus on these lighter moments. This will help establish a positive association with Hell Week. It will also help you sustain the momentum that you built up over the seven days. Of course, you will revert to your regular life in some ways. But you don't want to undergo a complete backslide, which is common with self-improvement regimens, especially health-based ones. You lose ten pounds only to gain back fifteen. Remember the holistic nature of mental training. The physical relates to the mental relates to the emotional. They support one another in a way that should prevent backsliding.

I once did Hell Week with the sales team at a midsize Nor-wegian manufacturer. Before our work started, each member of the team was averaging about fifteen calls per week. During Hell Week, the number of calls was upward of fifty—a huge uptick in production that was accomplished using all the tools discussed in this book, from time management to mode opti-mization. There was no way the team was going to maintain that pace indefinitely (as much as top management would have liked it). But I stayed on with the clients to help them keep the bar higher than it had been. Two months later, they were still averaging upward of thirty calls per week, or twice as many as when we started.

That's the kind of goal you should set for yourself in the first few months after Hell Week. I want to remind you of the fundamental philosophy of mental training: that through small incremental improvements in your life you can achieve mean-ingful change and have a better, more fulfilling existence. It's the small decisions that we make all day, every day, that define us as individuals. Remember this as you apply the lessons of Hell Week to your everyday life moving forward.

Let me also say a quick word about failure before moving on. Fear of failure is everywhere in the military version of Hell Week, where one false step can send you packing, but it's really not part of the vocabulary I bring to civilian Hell Week. If you didn't complete a task during Hell Week, that's not a failure. Rather, it's an opportunity to better understand your inner workings. Let's take the Thursday all-nighter. Though many of my clients rise to the challenge, there are those who find it impossible. I can remember one client in particular who had a demanding job and was worried that he wouldn't be able to pull his weight if he was up the entire night before. He didn't want to let his colleagues down, or incur the wrath of his manager. Those are valid concerns, but they also assumed a lot. For one thing, they assumed his performance would be diminished, when in fact people are often energized once they make it past dawn and into the actual workday. He also assumed that he'd be letting his colleagues down, which is a laudable thought, though what's to say it wouldn't have been a slower than normal day?

After talking about these various assumptions with my client after Hell Week, he came to recognize the extent to which he'd psyched himself out of the challenge without even giving it serious consideration. And the more he thought about it, the more he realized that he was often sabotaging his ambitions with similarly defeatist assumptions. In the end, the supposed Hell Week "failure" offered a real mental breakthrough moment for this client. With Hell Week still fresh in your mind, I want you to look for the same kinds of learning moments.

MAKE GOOD HABITS A HABIT

I also want you to continue to pay close attention to habits, since these require steady, constant commitment. People often say that it takes twenty-one days to create a new good habit or break an old bad one. I haven't seen any scientific proof of this, but I'll be very happy if you keep up your positive habits for the first three weeks after Hell Week—and then keep going for the three weeks after that.

Certain habits are especially important to monitor right after Hell Week. First on the list is exercise. I don't expect you to maintain ten sessions a week, but try to work out at least five times each week. That's a reasonable and realistic goal, even if you're someone who has never exercised regularly before.

Also, try to stick to a regular sleep pattern. Many people tell me this was one of the best takeaways from Hell Week, especially if they were in the habit of drinking alcohol most evenings or watching TV before bed. Those behavior patterns prevent your mind and body from enjoying true restorative sleep. So try to become a super healthy sleeper. I think you'll find your productivity will continue to go up.

Last, continue to maintain your appearance with careful grooming and wardrobe selection. I'm a big believer in the adage "Dress for the job you want, not the one you have." Hopefully it felt good walking out the door each morning looking like a million bucks. Let's keep that feeling going in the weeks to come.

IT'S ABOUT TIME

Time management is another major theme that should be at the top of your mind in the first phase after Hell Week. You should have identified key inefficiencies in your daily and weekly routines. Work diligently at correcting them in the days and weeks to come. Effective time management is a lot about habits, so it makes sense to focus on these two components together during this time.

How is it going with your daily to-do lists? Hopefully you established a routine in Hell Week that you will continue to work at and refine. If you've been doing them in the morning at the start of your workday, you might try doing them the night before, especially if the morning method hasn't been 100 percent effective. And are you succeeding in tackling the toughest items on your to-do list first? Remember how important this is to creating confidence and momentum for the day.

I also want you to keep close tabs on your weekly calendar during the initial post–Hell Week phase. The items on this calendar should reinforce your larger life goals, both personal and professional. Are you scheduling regular exercise into your weeks? Is there dedicated family time? If you're in a relationship, don't forget to make time for it. People who think that true romance has to be spontaneous aren't living in the real world. Life is busy! Make time for the important things.

Above all else, I want you to remember that self-improvement is a continuous process. Hell Week is designed to jump-start the process and give you a jolt of momentum. It's not going to fix every problem in your life or turn you into an overnight success. As time passes, you'll find that more lessons emerge. I was eighteen when I completed my first Hell Week, and more than two decades later, the experience is still with me. If I'm facing a fifteen-hour workday, I don't worry about fatigue, because I know I'm capable of going for much longer. Before a meeting with a challenging colleague or client, I simply think back on my most demanding officers. That's what Hell Week is all about—revealing your best self so that you can draw on it for the rest of your life.

THREE TO SIX MONTHS AFTER HELL WEEK

It is natural that, by this point, some of the good habits you developed during Hell Week will have begun to slip. Hell Week was an exercise, and just like any exercise, you cannot do it only once if you want to retain its effects. At this point, most people will find it is enough to revisit their Hell Week by meditating on their experiences from the week. Deeply thinking about and recalling how you felt, what you learned, and how you changed during Hell Week is calibrating yourself back onto the track of success.

Be careful not to romanticize the experience. This is one of the reasons people struggle to transition permanently into a highly productive lifestyle. It's fine to reminisce on the good times. But if that's the only thing you remember, you run the risk of living in a false past.

The healthy and helpful version of reminiscing is meditative remembering. It includes recalling the complexity of the past so that you can keep its lessons alive. If you are going to continue progressing, you will have to relive Hell Week. You will have to remember not just the rush of victory when you completed it, but also the tiredness, the discomfort, the feeling that you should abort your mission. You have to remember how hard it was if your memory of victory will be of any value to you.

Think back to Thursday of Hell Week, when you worked all day, then pushed through the night, and then powered through an effective and full Friday of work. Take some time before continuing with your reading to meditate on how difficult this was. Imagine yourself in the moment of most discomfort. Recall the painful feeling of every part of your body telling you to stop and give up. Once you have recalled these sensations, take time to remember the experience of getting into bed Friday night with deep satisfaction. Recalling these feelings will help you to revitalize your commitment to the concepts of Hell Week, because the reward was made sweet by the struggle itself.

Hell Week's day without sleep was only as effective as your ability to follow through with your plans. If you cheated, you won't have the inspiring memory of breaking your limits; it will just feel like you pushed them. This will also diminish how much you will gain from meditative recall. If you do not feel like you broke past your limits, I encourage you to either repeat Hell Week, or at least repeat the Thursday and Friday section of Hell Week. You need to have a moment in your life that you can look back to as a perfectly clear example of your ability to keep working until the job is done, regardless of discomfort and difficulty. You need a vivid memory of a successful Hell Week to make every week after it be a success.

KEEPING TIME

Before beginning Hell Week, you already knew that time management was key to success. Everybody knows a well-managed calendar is a step on the road to success that can't be skipped, but as a Hell Week veteran, you should know that there is much more to time management than that.

Most mildly successful people have used highly effective time management systems at some point in their life. Only a few have continued using time management for more than just the basics. The move from being mildly to highly successful can be maintained only with devotion to time management. Revisit the Wednesday sections on time management as needed. Carefully study your daily, weekly, monthly, and yearly planning techniques.

Plans are effective only when continually recalled. Your long-term plans should not be gathering dust. You should be reading them often. You also shouldn't be making plans for your week and then forgetting about them until it is time to execute them. You should be keeping them in mind, preparing for them, and readying yourself to ace planned tasks the second you get to them.

When you serve in the military, you are automatically more effective, because somebody else is planning out your time for you. You only have to concern yourself with performing your best, not with what to use your day on or when to complete an activity. All that is decided, and all that is left to do is work. You felt something similar to this during Hell Week. I told you what to think about each day, what to learn, and gave you specific tasks to complete. I told you when to sleep, when to get up, and how much you needed to exercise. This made it easier for you to focus on performing and pushing yourself.

My goal with this book is that you will notice how effective time management was when you had somebody else planning out much of your day. If you realize how much more effective you are when your day was planned out, when your focus was decided, and when you were regularly studying how to improve, you will realize you have to have this element in your life. I want you to come to these conclusions, because I cannot write a book long enough to guide you through the rest of your life, with daily focus areas, tasks, and goals.

Your success in the three-to-six-month period after Hell Week will be determined by your ability to do for yourself what I have done for you. If you do yourself the service of planning, you will be able to give current tasks everything you have. Until you can be consistent with planning and time management, it will be a struggle. But if you have been consistent up to now, you should start to feel that strong and effective habits are forming.

BACK TO FEEDBACK

If you have children, you will know that it is very difficult to see the changes in your child's growth from day to day. This is why we often find ourselves saying that children grow up before you know it. We often are not conscious of gradual change. We don't think we are aging either, until we find our first gray hair. Because you do not notice gradual change effectively, you have to employ the eyes and observations of those around you.

If you are going to be receptive to the feedback of others, you have to prepare by asking yourself how you have changed. First, ask yourself how you feel. How are you different from the person you were when you first opened this book? How were you different when you finished Hell Week? How are you different now, three months down the road? How will you be in three months from now, if you keep up what you have learned during Hell Week? Take some time to consider these questions and write down your answers. Then repeat the exercise. Consider each of these points again, preferably a day or two later. Write down your reflections again. This activity should bring you a great deal of satisfaction if you have been consistent in keeping up what you learned during Hell Week.

Now you should be well prepared for feedback from trusted friends and contacts. Prepare questions about yourself. Ask them what they consider to be your strong and weak sides. When they give you an answer, be respectful and thankful, and avoid getting offended or annoyed by any critical answers. These people are doing you a favor, and you cannot improve without learning about your weaknesses. Load yourself up with the good feedback you get, but look for the areas to improve more than anything. You should also be looking for areas where you have changed. This is why it can be beneficial to question some of the same people whom you consulted before or during Hell Week. They will be able to tell you about any changes they have observed in the past months.

IN THE MODE

Using mode-changing exercises should have brought you more calmness and confidence over the last months. In the three-to-six-month period after your Hell Week you will often feel discouraged as your old self pulls on your new self. You will want to return to old habits and ways. You will strongly feel the temptation to be lazy. Fight these inclinations by changing your mode appropriately.

Just like a pulled-together outfit is not accomplished with

one piece of clothing, getting into a work mode, play mode, or relaxation mode is not effectively accomplished with just one action. Mode calibration is one of the areas in which most people slip into bad habits by the three-month mark after Hell Week. It is easy to relapse into your old ways, telling yourself you have work to do and no time to worry about getting into the right mode. But all habits are hard to start and this one is no exception. If you work at it, mode control will eventually no longer be a bother, but will be as natural as breathing—which brings us to the first mode-changing activity: breathing.

To control your mode, remember to breathe deeply. Controlling your breathing is one of the simplest and easiest ways to improve your mood and shift yourself from a mode of fretting or worrying into a productive one where you are in full control. Breathing deliberately reminds you that you are living life purposefully and not by accident. You are in control. While steadying your breathing, imagine the task ahead and imagine doing it, completing it, and being satisfied.

Remember to use your posture to communicate to yourself and others that you are dedicated to the task ahead. This will mentally prepare you to do better and will tell others that you are professional and decisive. If you slouch or look at the floor, you will feel less inspired, and others will know it.

Communicate your confidence with your smile and demeanor. When you are walking down the street, stray smiles from friendly passersby can do wonders to lighten up your day. The smile is one of the simplest forms of communication, but it is also one of the most powerful. If you are not regularly smiling by the three-month mark, you need to change that now. It will make your next three months a lot easier.

ONE YEAR AFTER HELL WEEK

People who have gone through Hell Week often ask me if and when they should do one again. There's no single right answer to the question, except to say that it's time for another Hell Week when your life has developed enough slack, in the form of creeping bad habits or loss of focus, that it needs to be whipped back into shape. In my experience, this works out to roughly every twelve months or so, which is why I recommend an annual Hell Week. But that's meant to be a guideline, rather than a hard-and-fast rule. I have one client who does Hell Week every year right before his birthday as a way to frame the year to come. Another client with some pretty deep-seated health issues decided he needed to do Hell Week every six months. And I've worked with many people for whom just one Hell Week was enough, at least for now.

As you approach the one-year anniversary of your first Hell Week, I encourage you to put your life into fresh perspective, with at least the possibility of going through the experience again. A good starting point in the reflection process is to check back on the yearly plan you started during your initial

Hell Week, as well as the goals you set for yourself. How much does life today resemble the life you imagined all those months ago? Have you reached some or all of the goals you laid out? Or do you find you've slipped back into a state of complacency?

FINDING RENEWED MEANING

As you'll recall, one of the principal exercises of Hell Week is writing down the values that carry the most meaning in your life. While some of these values will be absolute, based on the way you were raised, the political affiliations you've developed, and the social circle you run in, I also believe in the evolution of a personal value system. That is to say, values change over time. The experience of Hell Week should have had a profound impact on your life, and so as you approach the one-year mark, I want you to reassess your list of key values.

Think back over the last twelve months. When were you the happiest? Which achievements made you the most proud? Answering these questions will help reveal the values that matter most at this particular juncture in your life. These core values, in turn, will lead to meaning, which I believe to be the single greatest indicator of fulfillment, satisfaction, and high performance. In the words of Steve Jobs, "The only way to do great work is to love what you do."

CHECK BACK IN WITH YOUR INNER DIALOGUE

During Hell Week, I also asked you to listen hard to your inner self and focus on the positive. How have you kept up that campaign? Have any negative voices crept back into your daily dialogue? As I've said many times in this book, people with a strong sense of personal conviction will outperform the doubters and naysayers every time. If your positive mind-set has started to waver, or if you detect an increase in energy leakages in your life, it's time to consider another Hell Week.

Now is the time to do a gut check on your resilience. In the military, Hell Week is all about toughness, both mental and physical. It's designed to weed out the weak so that what's left is an elite battle corps. My version of Hell Week is aimed at you the individual, but it uses the same "survival of the fittest" model, in that only your best and strongest habits and attributes make it through. Weeding out the negatives in your life should equip you with incredible resilience.

Is that the case? As you think back over the last year, have you taken on more challenges, in both your personal and professional lives? Has your risk tolerance gone up? Have you pushed the limits of what's possible and encouraged others around you to do the same? Remember the opening message of this book: *You can take a lot more than you think*.

That's been my life's mantra since the age of eighteen, when a man I'd never met before stood at the head of a class on survival training and dared a roomful of soldiers to believe what he said was true. Many among us would not believe. Some gave up that very same day. Others made it to the end of basic training before waving the white flag. And there were some who started Hell Week but didn't see it through to the other side. Finally, there were those of us who persevered. We proved our commander right by taking on more than we ever thought possible—and in doing so we took our lives to a whole new level.

My life has been propelled by that accomplishment ever since. Sure, there have been setbacks and downturns. I have experienced more failure than I care to admit. But each time, I've come back stronger, because I know what I'm capable of. My life's work has been to help others discover their best and truest selves. I've become the officer at the chalkboard daring people to take on more. And more. And more. In some cases, the result has been Olympic medals, championship trophies, and Fortune 500 awards. Other times, it's simply been a father learning how to spend more quality time with his children.

The rewards are nice, but the real fulfillment comes with knowing that you've pushed your life not just to the brink, but beyond it. That goal must always be your single focus and most relentless pursuit. And if, somehow, it does start to slip away, another Hell Week stands by to serve you.

ACKNOWLEDGMENTS

First and foremost, I would like to express my deepest gratitude to the Gallery Books team at Simon & Schuster. This book would not have been possible if it were not for the great support of Louise Burke, Jennifer Bergstrom, Jeremie Ruby-Strauss, Jennifer Robinson, Nina Cordes, and their entire group. You helped make this Norwegian author's biggest dream come true. I also would like to send my appreciation to Rebecca Paley for her unique talents and to Matt Jacobi for being the best right-hand man anyone could ever ask for.

I also am sincerely grateful to the United States of America. Thank you for giving me such a warm welcome. I have always had the highest respect for your country.

On a personal level, I want to acknowledge my parents, Gerd Bie and Sverre, for the values they instilled in me growing up. I truly honor them and hope to pass along their wisdom to our five wonderful children. I owe a huge thank-you to my father-in-law and dear friend, Trond Mohn, who has been and continues to be an inspiration to me.

Lastly, to all the people around the world who have read my books: I thank you for your time and devotion. I hope to continue to motivate you for many years to come.

Go For Godfølelse!